CUSTOM AND COMMAND

ENCOURAGEMENT FROM THE SCRIPTURES
FOR AN UNUSUAL NEW BREED OF CHRISTIANS

- WITH SOME ANSWERS FOR THOSE WHO MIGHT FEEL
CRITICAL OF THEM

Stan Firth

Published by J.S.Firth

LONDON

© 1996 J. S. Firth

Reprinted: February 1998
Second Reprint: August 1999

Printed by: *SPEEDPRINT*
              Gladiator Works
              Gladiator Street
              London SE23 1NA
              Tel: 0181 690 8282

CONTENTS

Page

PART ONE - INTRODUCTION.

| Chapter | 1. | An unstructured Church-Lifestyle | 6 |
| Chapter | 2. | Why? | 9 |

PART TWO - GATHERINGS FOR WORSHIP: A FRESH LOOK AT THE BIBLE.

Chapter	3.	Some surprises in both Old and New Testaments...	14
Chapter	4.	"Assembling ourselves together" - and other challenges...	18
Chapter	5.	"Custom and Command"	21
Chapter	6.	Believers at Worship	23
Chapter	7.	Singing to the Lord	27

PART THREE - OTHER CHURCH ACTIVITIES, FROM THE BIBLE'S VIEWPOINT.

Chapter	8.	Two Worthy Ways of Teaching	31
Chapter	9.	Practicalities of Teaching - Then and Now	35
Chapter	10.	The Task which Follows the Teaching. (Christian Service)	39
Chapter	11.	Does "Informal" = "Ineffective"?	42
Chapter	12.	Keeping Organisation in its Proper Place	45
Chapter	13.	Leadership is Low Key, but Liberating	48
Chapter	14.	Leadership and Authority	51

PART FOUR - DEALING WITH PEOPLE'S PRACTICAL RESERVATIONS.

Chapter	15.	Maintaining the Motivation?	55
Chapter	16.	Involved in Fruitfulness?	61
Chapter	17.	A Vision of the Body-of-Christ?	66

ACKNOWLEDGEMENTS

I would like to put on record my gratitude to David Rice for undertaking the demanding task of preparing the manuscript for printing; and to Robert Stockwell for the painstaking job of reading the proofs.

Then there is a widely scattered group of people who read my first draft, made helpful comments and suggestions, and urged me to go to print. To all of them I express my very sincere thanks for their time and encouragement.

In addition I am indebted to several warm-hearted people who have contributed towards the financial cost of making the booklet available more widely than we could ever have done on our own.

Acknowledgement is due, also, to those who have been an inspiration to me. There is John Beaumont, whose prophetic books and personal conversations first led me to consider the Christian lifestyle described in these pages.

I owe a lot, also, to families and individuals whose living-out of that lifestyle I have been privileged to observe over a number of years; and the other pioneers of the lifestyle with whom I have been able to correspond, even when some of them lived ten thousand miles away! The list is long. I wouldn't know where to draw the line if I started to mention names.

Let me mention Mavis, my wife, however. Over the years we have always been together in asking the Lord what He wanted of us. She has shared at every turn in the process of "keeping in step with the Spirit" which has led, among other things, to the writing of "Custom and Command".

S.F. 1/11/1996

PART ONE

INTRODUCTION

Chapter 1
An Unstructured Church-Lifestyle

Over the last five years I have been increasingly coming across something quite new in my Christian experience: believers who are indisputably enthusiastic about Jesus Christ, and about serving Him in the world, but who no longer "go to church"! They have given up the practice of regular corporate worship and are not engaged in the usual church activities. It is impossible, however, to categorise them as "backsliders", for they continue in their personal devotion to Christ, and seem to display the generally accepted characteristics of Christian discipleship - except in the whole area of church life.

It is possible that you have not yet come across believers who could be described in this way; but as an increasing number of Christians are making this change, the probability is that you have met one or two at least - or soon will do! Such an encounter usually provokes one of three reactions: some people are highly critical of such a departure from normal Christian practice; others are delighted and start moving in this unusual lifestyle themselves; others again are just confused - as I was for several years.

For quite some time I asked myself what I should make of this unusual new breed of Christians. Were they a harmless minority lifestyle which could safely be left to co-exist alongside the other churches? On the other hand, did they represent a dangerous trend, against which other Christians should be warned? Or could it be that they had something to say to the Church in general? At first, I really didn't know what to think, though I had my own specific reasons for wanting to find out, (which I shall explain in the next chapter).

As time passed, I got the opportunity to question a fair number of such Christians, from various parts of the world, about their attitude to Church. All seemed to reply in similar vein: "We consider the Church of Jesus Christ to be vitally important, both world-wide and locally, but we see it as **unstructured rather than structured.** We believe our calling is to an UNSTRUCTURED CHURCH LIFESTYLE."

For a considerable period I found that the idea of "unstructured church lifestyle" was not a concept I could even begin to grasp! However, one day I thought of an experience in my own life - one which lasted several years - which gave me a kind of analogy for "unstructured church life". From then on I could *understand* what the "unstructured Christians" were doing. Whether I could *approve* of what they were doing would need further consideration, but at least I now knew what their outlook was.

Whether you are already involved in an "unstructured church lifestyle", or dead set against it, or simply feeling your way in the whole issue, I believe this analogy will be of some use to you:

* * * * * * * * * * *

For a number of years I was a teacher in a London Comprehensive School. One of the things I specially liked about my time at that school was that there was a good sprinkling of teachers on the staff who were committed Christians. As Christians we seemed to relate together well. (Now that many of us have gone our separate ways, we still keep in touch.)

There was nothing formal about how we related. We didn't "hold meetings", yet we frequently met together. Only occasionally would the whole crowd be in the one place at the one time, and there was no regularity or predictability about that - though I do remember a spell of about three weeks when as many as possible used to meet every lunch-hour. (One of our number had gone, with his wife, as an exchange teacher to Australia. While there, the wife was stricken with a life-threatening illness. Each evening someone from our group would get news through the couple's parents in Wales, so the next day at 12.30 we would gather to hear the latest, and to pray. These prayers, part of a volume of prayer from many places, were answered "much more than we could ask or think" - but that is another story.)

We did feel a strong compulsion to care for one another and to encourage one another to live out our Christian lives effectively in the school environment. We chatted often; sometimes in twos or threes, sometimes in slightly larger numbers in one of the classrooms (usually Room 9!) or sometimes, of an evening, in someone's home. I can honestly say that I don't think we were a "clique", yet we were a "body" within the school community. There was plenty of inter-relating with the staff in general, yet we definitely had an awareness of the responsibilities (and privileges) of our Christian fellowship.

Looking back, I can see abundant "fruit" from the links that were built between us: we were helped to do our job better; we were helped in our personal lives; we were deepened by each other in our understanding of the Scriptures and of God's purposes for us; and there were young people (pupils) who came to faith, and were matured spiritually, through the relationships they had with the Christian teachers.

We weren't an organisation - just a **loose association** of Christian teachers in that particular school community. Towards the end of my time there, I discovered that what we had going had a nation-wide counterpart called "A.C.T." (Association of Christian Teachers). They had a little bit more structure about them than we had, but not a lot. They didn't hold regular meetings -just "ad hoc" ones when a particular issue which affected Christian teachers needed an airing, or when a speaker, with something to say of special value to Christians in the profession, was in the area. Their literature was very helpful, Among other things, it made me realise that the kind of fellowship which we had in our school could be found in countless other establishments. Our local "loose association" was just a small part of something much much wider in educational circles.

* * * * * * * * * * * *

When all this came to my recollection, while I was trying to get to grips with what the advocates of "unstructured church life" were saying, I suddenly saw what they were on about! They believed their calling was much more to a "loose association" of Christians in each locality, than to something organised and structured like the usual churches or fellowships. They were not isolated Christians "doing their own thing", as I had at first imagined. They did have a sense of church - but not of church as I had always known it, with its set meeting-places and meeting-times, its organisations and its activities. Their vision was of Christians relating to one another within a geographical area, in much the same way as we teachers had related to one another within the more limited community of our school. I also realised that, just as there was a nation-wide dimension to our "loose association" at the High School, so there was an international or world-wide dimension to the network of seemingly unattached believers which was developing.

Could this kind of church-lifestyle, so different from any other, possibly have any Biblical validity? When news began to filter through that some Christians were abandoning the well-worn paths of church-practice, I heard many people saying words to this effect: "A 'loose association'! Well, that's certainly well out of line with *my* idea of Church!"

For my own part, however, I could not dismiss this matter quite so easily. It was not sufficient for me that this was out of line with centuries of Christian thinking. That was what people said at the beginning of almost every positive development in Church history! That it should be out of line with *my* idea of church, or anyone else's idea of church, seemed to me of no great consequence. **But was it really out of line with God's idea of Church?** That, to me, was the issue which needed weighing up, if Christians were properly to assess this new style of church life which was increasingly being practised.

There was only one thing for it - to re-examine the Scriptures on the whole matter....

CHAPTER 2
WHY?

Before I turn directly to the Scriptures, however, I want to give something of an explanation (quite brief, at this stage) as to why earnest Christians should want to adopt this alternative church lifestyle.

Some of them would say simply: "God has called us to this." Although it is certainly possible for some people to mistake a "bee in their bonnet" for the voice of the Lord, I have learned to respect Christians with a strong sense of call from God. This respect dates from many years ago, when, as a young man, I heard the tiny Gladys Aylward speak in Aberdeen. (You remember Gladys, the humble domestic servant whom the Missionary Societies rejected. So strong was her sense of call to China that, branded as naive by everyone else, she set out by herself, via the Trans-Siberian Railway, and did years of sterling service in the Far East, for which she was eventually held in high honour.)

With regard to this new departure in church life, I have had letters and verbal accounts from various people in different parts of the globe who witness to a call from God something like Gladys's - or like Abraham's, when he was called to leave the familiar surroundings of Ur and go out into the unknown. It has not been easy - especially if, to begin with, they have known of no-one else of like mind. These folks have felt the strongest possible compulsion to leave the familiar surroundings of church life, and venture into this, as yet, largely uncharted lifestyle!

There are others, however, who might explain their changeover in terms of a "growing conviction" (which can be, of course, another way the Lord calls His followers). Some of those I have encountered were increasingly finding that Christian responses, which they felt important, were being hindered, rather than helped, by the way most churches are organised. If that sounds a bit vague, and you're not really sure what they meant by such a complaint, I believe I can best illustrate it by recounting a couple of similar situations which were experienced by my wife, Mavis, and myself.

* * * * * * * * * * *

Most Christians would agree that the outward activity which Jesus wants of His followers is to bless others. "Love the Lord your God... is the first and greatest commandment... and the second is like it: love your neighbour... All the Law and the prophets hang on these two commandments." (Matthew 22:37-40) "Blessing others" in Jesus' teaching, means a wide range of actions through the whole spectrum from "giving a cup of cold water" to "making disciples from all nations". (There's more about all this in chapter 10.)

Now, Mavis and I have always believed that the principal way of blessing others is PERSON TO PERSON, and that the setting up of PROJECTS to bless others, though definitely sometimes valid, is secondary to the Christian's duty to relate in some depth to the individuals he or she comes across in the normal course of life.

Thirty years ago we consciously adopted a little motto: "PEOPLE MATTER MORE THAN PROJECTS". Sadly, we have allowed that motto to be obscured from time to time in our Christian service. Though this was our own fault, it has to be said that church life, as we have known it, worked against the motto. We found that there were so many meetings, organisations and responsibilities, that there was very little time to relate to other people except superficially - especially those outside the church circle. We felt that we (and, we suspect, many, many other church people) were like the priest and the Levite on the Jericho road: too busy hurrying to and from church work to notice, or get involved with, someone in real need. At one stage we tried to be good members of our church without going to all the during-the-week activities others expected - but we definitely felt "out of it".

When, therefore, we heard of a church-lifestyle which would give us the support of other Christians, and yet would leave us free to be much more involved with other people, both committed and uncommitted, we naturally pricked up our ears. We knew, of course, that greater freedom in one area of the Christian life alone could never be sufficient reason for us to make this major change-over others had made. And we knew also that the whole thing would need to be checked out against Scripture - but it did help us to understand the new freedom others were claiming to find.

*   *   *   *   *   *   *   *   *   *   *

Another scriptural truth which has often seemed hampered by church-life, as we have experienced it, is expressed by Jesus to Nicodemus in John 3:8: "The wind blows wherever it pleases. You hear its sound, but you cannot tell where it comes from or where it is going. So it is with everyone born of the Spirit." Jesus seems to be teaching that we should be non-predictable in life (not un-predictable, by the way). But the lives of a great many Christians are very "time-tabled" by the weekly list of church activities, and therefore very predictable! Whereas the Spirit of God seems to want believers who are available to meet a whole range of real needs as they arise, we always seem to have found ourselves in a strait-jacket imposed by our diaries. Once again, the "unstructured church-lifestyle", of which some of our friends were speaking, offered a refreshing freedom to do God's will as we understood it.

I could go on and on about those elements which we felt were a genuine part of God's purpose for us, but which were hampered by church structures. It had been a problem for us all through life, and had twice caused us to change denomination, (an amazingly common happening nowadays, we note, among serious-minded Christians!) But the unstructured church could not be the answer for us, unless it was in line with God's idea of Church, as revealed in the Scriptures. Even though we have no warmth towards a legalistic "political correctness" in Christian things, we do absolutely believe that any so-called leading from God must be consistent with Biblical principles in the matter.

So I set about examining the Bible very closely on the subject of church life. I FOUND THE SCRIPTURES TO BE STUNNINGLY SUPPORTIVE OF AN UNSTRUCTURED CHURCH- LIFESTYLE!

If you don't believe that, I would respectfully ask you to read on - especially if you have been inclined to use words like "heresy" and "error" about Christians who have gone over to these ways. If you have adopted a hostile position, it cannot be a strong one, if you brush possible contrary evidence under the carpet. You can only be strong in your Christian opinions if you consider Biblical viewpoints which others put forward, and can demonstrate their weakness. That is all I am asking you to do: to consider the Scriptures again, on the matter of church lifestyle.

Incidentally, in saying "the Scriptures are stunningly supportive of an unstructured church lifestyle" I am not at all saying that the Scriptures are against all other church lifestyles. Whoever you are, reading this booklet, be assured that it is no part of my purpose to attack your, or anyone's, church lifestyle. I merely want to point out that **the "unstructured" lifestyle is well within the guidelines for church life laid down in Scripture - contrary to what I at first expected.** I suspect you, the reader, may share something of my progressive amazement as the relevant biblical passages unfold.

You have probably guessed by now that Mavis and I have, in fact, linked up with this "new breed of Christians" (as I called them on the title page). We have left the Fellowship to which we have belonged for ten years, and indeed the whole "structured church" scene to which we have belonged, as adults, for more or less forty years! We did so when we reached the double conviction: a) that only in this way can we live out the particular responses to Christ which He has laid on our hearts (much more of this, with regard to ourselves *and* others, as we go on, and especially in the final chapter); and b) that, contrary to what most Christians seem to imagine; the Scriptures do not raise objections to this kind of lifestyle.

* * * * * * * * * * * *

This chapter was entitled "Why?" In one sense that meant: "Why on earth would some Christians, who in other respects seem reasonably orthodox, want to abandon the centuries-old traditions of church life?" I hope I have at least begun to point the way to an answer - and more reasons will emerge, especially in the concluding section of the whole book.

In another sense, however, the "Why?" of the chapter heading meant: "Why did I write this book?" - and the answer to that is two-fold: I wrote firstly, to explain ourselves to many dear personal friends - people who honour the guidance of the Bible, and were bound to be startled, initially, by this development in our Christian lives. We intended that they should be re-assured that we continue to walk in God's ways, though our pathway is different from theirs. (I did not set out to convert them to our ways; only to quell their fears for us.)

This "explaining of things" was meant, originally, for people who were known to us personally. However I have been encouraged to make it available to a wider readership, so that it might help explain things to folks who are unknown to us.

The other - equally important - reason for writing, is to encourage fellow Christians who have left the long accepted structures (whether they were traditional denominational churches or the newer "charismatic" fellowships). I have gone through the Scriptures very carefully, to be sure that we are within God's order. I wanted to share with other believers who have "cut loose", because I found the results of my studies so affirming and heart-warming. Once again, I have been urged to make the book generally available outside the structures - well beyond our own circle of friends.

* * * * * * * * * * * *

When the "unstructured church" - this "loose association" concept - first comes to the notice of other Christians, there are numerous areas of doubt which crowd into their heads, for example, "What about regular meeting together?" "What about worship?" "What about systematic teaching?" "What about leadership? "What about co-ordinated outreach and service in the community?" "With regard to fellowship, isn't this 'informal fellowship' too much of a 'hit and miss' affair?" and so on.

I set myself to examine in detail what exactly the Scriptures had to say about all of these topics, and the results of my investigations are contained in the next two sections of the book. Part Two deals with what may seem, to many Christians, to be the central issue: Regular Corporate Worship. Part Three deals with the other aspects of church life.

One last thought for this chapter: **I must stress that this book is for the man or woman who values Biblical guidelines, and is willing to *ponder* them from time to time.** If you are looking for an undemanding "book at bedtime", or for something you can "skim-read", this is not the reading material for you! It is intended to be a serious (but, I hope, refreshing) attempt to look at what the Bible says about the basic foundations of church life.

PART II

GATHERINGS FOR WORSHIP

- A FRESH LOOK AT THE BIBLE

CHAPTER 3

SOME SURPRISES IN BOTH OLD AND NEW TESTAMENTS

When I began to study the Word of God in earnest about this particular matter, I got quite a few surprises, even in the Old Testament! Here's the first surprise: corporate worship wasn't in operation at all until the Tabernacle was constructed for use by the Israelites during their forty years in the wilderness. None of the early Old Testament figures "went to church"! (Yet who can doubt the devotion of Noah, Abraham, Isaac, Jacob, or Joseph?)

When the Tabernacle stopped travelling, and became a fixed building, corporate worship was confined to one site, and one site only, in the whole of Israel. (Shiloh first - where young Samuel served; then a brief spell at Nob; and finally Jerusalem, where Solomon "up-graded" it into his magnificent Temple.) So, here was another surprise: if, during those hundreds of years, you didn't live in the part of the land where the *only* worship-centre was, then you just didn't go to corporate worship at all, unless of course, like Samuel's mother Hannah, you paid the occasional visit.

THE FACT IS THAT, FOR MOST OF THE OLD TESTAMENT ERA, CORPORATE WORSHIP WAS ONLY AVAILABLE WHEN THERE WAS A TABERNACLE / TEMPLE, AND FOR THOSE WHO LIVED NEAR ENOUGH TO GO TO THE TEMPLE.

In the light of these facts, we have to ask ourselves about the meaning of the fourth commandment: "Remember the Sabbath Day - to keep it holy". Could it really always have meant "Go to corporate worship every Saturday", if the facilities were not available for most people much of the time? An examination of the Biblical references to "sabbath-breaking" will show that any complaint was always about working; continuing to do business on the rest-day God had said should be "set apart" (the same word as "holy"). Nothing ever seems to be said about worship being missed! (Look at Nehemiah 13: 15-22, for instance).

In the last couple of centuries BC., of course, the custom grew up of having local synagogues with regular services every Sabbath. But here is yet another surprise: This came about without any command from God, so far as what is reported in the Bible is concerned! It doesn't seem likely that the Scriptures would say *nothing*, if such an important feature had been introduced as a result of something the Lord God had expressed. (Books like the IVP "New Bible Dictionary", or any history of Israel, would confirm this late, humanly initiated, development in Jewish culture.)

Nonetheless, by the beginning of the Christian era, corporate worship, in particular buildings, at set hours, was, for the first time, firmly established among the Jews. AMAZINGLY, HOWEVER, THE NEW TESTAMENT MAKES NO

ATTEMPT TO COMMEND THE CONTINUANCE OF THIS PATTERN IN CHRISTIAN FORM!

* * * * * * * * * * *

The New Testament seems to have had little enthusiasm for set times and places of worship. We'll look at places first. The early Christian leaders spoke against the idea of having particular buildings that you might call "God's House" or "the Sanctuary", (although the term had been used of the Temple in Jerusalem).

Stephen proclaimed (Acts 7:48-49): "**The Most High does not live in houses made by men.** As the prophet says 'Heaven is my throne and the earth my footstool. What kind of house will you build for me, says the Lord'" (He was quoting Isaiah 66:1) Later on Paul preached (Acts 17:24): "**The God who made the world and everything in it does not live in temples built by hands.**"

For the first three centuries AD the Christians listened to that advice, and then, at the beginning of the fourth century, when the Emperor Constantine became a Christian and Christianity became the "done thing", the buildings started to appear, and the Church reverted to the late Jewish pattern.

Another early Christian leader who does not seem to have had much enthusiasm for "meeting-houses", or for the organising of worship, was the writer to the Hebrews. He points out (Hebrews 9:1): "Now **the *first* covenant had regulations for worship, and also an earthly sanctuary**". I don't think it is unreasonable to suggest that he is implying that the New Covenant, under which we live, does not have either!

* * * * * * * * * * *

At first sight, this doing away with an earthly sanctuary, or a building which you can call the "House of God" seems to make some of the lovely verses from the Psalms almost meaningless - verses about the importance of God's House - some of them engraved on our hearts through the singing of Christian psalms-and-hymns-and-spiritual-songs. For example:
"How Lovely is Thy dwelling place, O Lord of Hosts to me" (Ps 84 v 1)
"I would rather be a doorkeeper in the House of our God than to dwell in the tents of the wicked" (Ps 84 v10)
"The righteous will flourish like a palm tree.... Planted in the House of the Lord. They will flourish in the courts of our God." (Ps 92 v 12-13)
"We are filled with the good things of Your House ... of your Holy Temple" (Ps 65 v 4)
"I was glad, very glad, when they said to me,
Let us go to the House of the Lord today" (Ps 122 v 1 Scripture in Song)
"O enter then His gates with praise

Approach with joy His courts unto" (Ps 100 v 1 Metrical Psalm version)
"Come bless the Lord, all ye servants of the Lord
Who stand by night in the House of the Lord" (Ps 134 v1 Scripture in Song)

There are many more "House-of-God" verses. Have they all to be 'ditched' by those outside the structures?

Not at all! I would suggest to you that a key to their meaning for New Testament believers lies in 1 Peter 2:5 "You also as living stones are being built into a spiritual house"

"Our local house-of-God", those of us who have left the structures would tend to say, "is not one of bricks and mortar". Nor is it one of organisational arrangements. The house-of-God we belong to is one of *relationships* - relationships with the Lord and relationships with each other. WHAT HAS BEEN CALLED A "LOOSE ASSOCIATION" IS, IN FACT **A HOUSE OF LIVING STONES.**

These "House-Of-God" verses remain meaningful for us. We *do* think that our loose association, our house-of-living-stones is lovely. We don't mind if we seem unspectacular as Christians - mere doorkeepers - so long as we are participants in a house of living stones. We are grateful that we are not 'loners' but that, for us, the roots of our spirits are planted into a group of believers. That keeps us flourishing! We *are* filled with good things that flow from the House of Living Stones. We *are* glad - very glad - when any kind of linking-up with our fellow-believers, however informal, is suggested. When we do link up it *does* call forth praise from our hearts. What the Psalmist felt about the Temple, *we* feel about our House Of Living Stones, our loose association of believers.

That phrase from 1 Peter 2:5 - "spiritual house of living stones" - will reappear many times in the course of this book. This is not because I want to base a whole doctrine on a few words picked out of an isolated verse (though, sadly, that kind of thing has often been done in the past). I am emphasising the verse simply because it seems to me that it sums up the entire drift of the New Testament scriptures on the subject of church life. The New Testament speaks of a church which is nothing more and nothing less than a grouping of Christians built and held together, not by a stone mason, nor by an organiser or administrator, but by the Spirit. That is the kind of House of God to which those of us "outside the structures" belong, and which we so greatly appreciate

* * * * * * * * * * *

So much for the subject of set places of worship. There is also the question of *set times and Sunday meetings!* I've sifted through all the references I can find to "the Lord's Day" and "the first day of the week", and can only find two occasions when it was specifically said that a gathering of God's people was on a Sunday - and in neither case is there any mention of gathering for worship! The first was in Acts 2, verse 1, where the followers of Jesus were "all together in one place" on the Day of Pentecost (which was always a Sunday, not a Sabbath). It doesn't say what they had come together for, but, over a period, they had been meeting "constantly" (daily?) for prayer (reminding me of the daily prayer times our "loose association" had, at school, when our colleague's wife was so ill). So, the gathering may have been part of this phase of special prayer - although it should be mentioned that that particular day was a national day of celebration, the kind of day family and friends get together anyway. The other occasion was in Acts 20 verse 7 where Paul gives the believers in Ephesus a lengthy teaching session the night before he is due to leave the district

It is true that the apostle John had a great spiritual experience on a Sunday, but he was under arrest at the time, and makes no mention of the presence of others. (Revelation 1:9-10). Paul suggests that Sunday, being the first day of the week, is a good day to lay aside something from your wages for those in need (1 Corinthians 16:2) - but there is no mention of a "Sunday meeting" being involved.

And that's about it. Apart from these references, Sunday isn't mentioned in the New Testament!

What I've been pointing out in this chapter doesn't mean, as I'll be explaining shortly, that there is anything necessarily *wrong* with turning up for worship at a set time on a Sunday, at a particular building. All I am asking is: Please don't say that the Bible **commands** it, or even that the Bible **commends** it.

CHAPTER 4

ASSEMBLING OURSELVES TOGETHER, AND OTHER CHALLENGES

There are, of course, quite a few other references in the New Testament to "gatherings" or "get-togethers" of Christians. Because they don't mention Sunday or Corporate Worship doesn't mean that we can overlook them. There is, for instance, the famous verse most often brought up in discussions about the unstructured church lifestyle: **"Forsake not the assembling of yourselves together, as the manner of some is"** (Hebrews 10:25 AV). The first thing I would point out, with regard to this verse, is the context - which shows what the writer was expecting to happen at these get-togethers. It wasn't worship! It was: "Consider how we may spur one another on to love and good works" (v24); and "Let us encourage one another" (v25). It wasn't even a teaching session; it was a time for conversation among people.

The second issue I would want to point out with regard to Hebrews 10:25 is that critics of unstructured church-life always seem to quote this verse from the Authorised Version, even though many of them don't actually use the AV much. Whereas most translations say "meeting together", the AV says "assembling together", which sounds a little grander, and perhaps gives the impression that we ought to be at something which is like a school assembly, or a Christian Brethren assembly.

The truth is, however, that the actual Greek verb (epi-sun-ag-ein), translated as "assemble together" in the AV simply means "to gather together" - of any numbers, including small numbers. Jesus used the selfsame word when talking about vultures gathering round a dead body (Luke 17:37). You don't get many vultures round one corpse - usually just a pair, or a couple of pairs! Jesus also uses that actual word to describe the hen gathering her chicks under her wings (Matthew 23:37). You don't get all that many chickens under one mother hen!

So, it really is a bit naughty to use this verse to suggest that we ought to be at regular occasions which have the characteristics of "assemblies", and that when we get there, we should be engaging in corporate worship. The verse itself doesn't carry either of these implications. In fact, with regard to numbers, there is absolutely no reason why it could not refer to an informal get-together of, say, two couples or half-a-dozen individuals. All the verse really means is: "It is essential to have get-togethers with other Christians for mutual encouragement and spurring-on to good works. The living stones of a spiritual house are not to remain isolated. They are to be linked with each other. They are constantly to develop relationships with one another.

* * * * * * * * * * * *

The other often-quoted passage is in 1 Corinthians chapter 14, especially perhaps verses 24 to 26: "**If an unbeliever.... comes in while <u>everybody</u> is prophesying, he will be convinced by all that he is a sinner... and the secrets of his heart will be laid bare.** So he will fall down and <u>worship</u> God, exclaiming, 'God is really among you!'.... When you come together <u>everyone</u> has a hymn, or a word of instruction, a revelation, a tongue or an interpretation. **All of these must be done for the strengthening of the church.**" I have put some underlinings within the actual quotation because these verses clearly envisage quite a few people, including "outsiders", meeting together. There is mention of worship (at least by the new convert) and there is certainly singing.

But look at the verse immediately before all this - verse 23. Paul introduces the whole section by saying: "**<u>If</u> the whole church comes together...**". "<u>IF</u>" - not "When"! "<u>IF</u>" not "Each Sunday"! Absolutely all the translations, from the AV onwards, agree that the word is IF. In other words, Paul doesn't seem to envisage all the Christians of the local House of Living Stones coming together with regularity - but if they do, we may expect the kind of thing he outlines.

THE SECOND HALF OF 1 CORINTHIANS Ch.14 IS ABOUT THE CHARACTERISTICS OF AN OCCASIONAL, NON-REGULAR GATHERING OF THE WHOLE LOCAL BODY, AND NOT AT ALL ABOUT SOMETHING REGULAR AND FREQUENT!

* * * * * * * * * * * *

A small digression here, for those who specially value the concept of "Body Ministry". If you have no particular interest, you can skip this bit until the next set of asterisks!

"Body Ministry Worship" is exactly what is going on in 1 Corinthians chapter 14. Now, "Body Ministry" - where everyone has their part to play - can be a genuinely lovely part of Christian experience in all sorts of ways. But Mavis and I have found that, so far as people worshipping together is concerned, it quickly loses its spontaneity and gets into ruts, if it becomes regular and frequent. The only way it keeps its freshness, at least according to our observation, is if it maintains the qualities of occasional-ness and non-regularity - which is exactly what Paul seems to have in mind when he says "<u>If</u> the whole church comes together..."

Incidentally, in my writing-out-by-hand of this booklet, I had reached the end of the last paragraph. The following day, we went to quite a sizeable gathering, in someone's house, for Christians in our locality who had experienced this "drawing-away-from-structured-church-life" I described earlier. It would have been perfectly acceptable for this occasion to have been nothing more than a "get-together on a fuller scale" of these Christians but, as it turned out, the gathering did have the refreshing "body-ministry" qualities of the passage we've been discussing. That this should happen at exactly this point in my writing seemed to us a remarkable confirmation of the point I had been trying to make.

* * * * * * * * * * * *

Let me revert, however, to the main issue. We have been looking, in this chapter and the previous one, at New Testament gatherings of Christians which have been superficially, but inaccurately, accepted as examples of regular corporate worship. There are, of course, other references in the New Testament to gatherings of Christians. We shall be dealing with these in later chapters. But, as we shall see, these other passages refer to non-worship reasons for Christians getting together, and they certainly give no hint of anything like sticking to set times each week.

To conclude this line of argument: **It does not seem as if there was either a doctrine or a practice of regular corporate worship in the Early Church! If you think otherwise, then there is an onus upon you to produce the evidence from the pages of Scripture!** (And it needs to be something a bit stronger than a few superficial comments about "forsaking the assembling of ourselves together" or about 1 Corinthians 14.)

THE TRUTH IS THAT THE BIBLE'S TEACHING ON THE WHOLE SUBJECT IS THE EXACT OPPOSITE OF WHAT MOST CHRISTIANS THINK. THERE IS NO URGING TO BE AT CORPORATE WORSHIP, EACH SUNDAY, IN SOME KIND OF "SANCTUARY", ANCIENT OR MODERN!

* * * * * * * * * * * *

Does this mean that centuries of church-goers have been wrong? Not at all - as I shall hope to demonstrate in the next chapter. Does this mean that I have to brand as "heretics" everyone nowadays who goes faithfully to Sunday worship, or that I have to cut myself off from loving fellowship with them? In no way - as the next stage of my booklet will reveal. But it does mean that my "fellow travellers", and I, should not be branded as heretics either, since we are not, after all, out of harmony with the Scriptures. Those who are associated with the "unstructured church" must not let their good be evil spoken of. They can hold their heads up high and say: "I am walking with the Lord, in the light of His word - within the bounds of Scripture."

CHAPTER 5

CUSTOM AND COMMAND

At this juncture I want to introduce a way of putting things which I find helpful. I call it "Custom and Command" and I think it is so important that I have used this expression as the overall title for the whole book. If I take a little time to explain the thing, please bear with me. **I believe the explanation is absolutely crucial in the whole issue, and the only hope of avoiding the disunity which, sadly, breaks out all too easily among Christians.**

There are certain features of the life of God's people which are in existence because of **commands** of God. If something is specifically instructed in Scripture, we must include it in our lifestyle; if something is specifically banned, we must exclude it. But, there are features also which are **customs** - ways of doing things which are introduced because they seem, at the time, to be helpful to an individual believer or to the life of a Community of God's People.

God does not disown our customs - unless of course they are quite contrary to something He has expressly instructed, or unless He has made absolutely clear to us that the time to discontinue the custom has come.

The Synagogue is a good example of this. God did not institute it, yet the Bible tells us that it was the "custom" of Jesus to go there every Sabbath (Luke 4:16). Of course, later on, after a period when Christian converts were often won in the synagogues, the Spirit of Jesus did lead the Christians to discontinue the custom. (Even in Jesus' lifetime He was beginning to dissociate Himself from the Synagogue: in Matthew 10:17 He says "Be on your guard... they will flog you in their synagogues" - *their* synagogues; no longer *our* synagogues.) All the same, the fact is that both the Son and the Spirit worked through the Synagogue, even if it was a "custom" rather than a "command".

Sometimes the Scriptures use words which are similar to the word "custom", e.g. "practices" or "traditions". Now a **practice** isn't a God-given **principle.** It is a way things are appropriately done, at the time, by the believers. You remember that the first Christian women used to cover their heads, or veil themselves, if they were praying in the presence of menfolk. Actually, Paul is quite keen on this procedure, but he describes it as a "practice" (1 Corinthians 11:16). By using the word "practice" he didn't elevate the matter into a "principle" - so it's quite in order that many 20th-century Christian women have discontinued the practice. If it had been a principle, it couldn't have been ignored. Do you agree that there is a clear distinction between Custom and Command; between Practice and Principle?

In the same way, - to continue the alliteration so well-loved by many preachers! - **Traditions aren't Torah** (the Jewish name for God's Law). That is where Jesus took issue with the Pharisees. They didn't distinguish clearly between what *God* had actually laid down, and what they themselves had decided to do. They began to confuse their own centuries-old traditions with the Torah - the Commands of Almighty God! Jesus came to be the fulfilment of the Law (the Torah) - but not to be a fulfilment of the traditions. Yet the Pharisees found fault with Him because He didn't fulfil the traditions as well!

* * * * * * * * * * * *

I BELIEVE THAT REGULAR-SUNDAY-CORPORATE-WORSHIP IS A **CUSTOM**, A CENTURIES-OLD TRADITION, BUT IT IS NOT A **COMMAND**. As I have tried to illustrate from the pages of the Bible, it does not feature anything like as largely in Scripture as most believers imagine. It is not urged upon Christians as they seem to think!

Nevertheless, just as some great things happened through the custom of having Synagogues, so great things have happened, down through the ages, and in present times, through the whole set-up centred round Sunday worship. If you are a regular Sunday worshipper and an enthusiastic member of a local "structured" fellowship, there is no reason why you should discontinue your custom, unless, of course, God were to bring a contrary conviction to you.

But, by the same token, you mustn't take a Pharisee's view, and confuse your custom with God's commands - so that you frown and "tut-tut" about brothers and sisters who are no longer walking in your traditions!

* * * * * * * * * * * *

I feel warmly towards *anyone* who loves the Lord Jesus Christ, and shows it by seeking to live under His Lordship; anyone who desires to serve and bless fellow-humans, in Jesus' name. I would think it wrong to let their *traditions* stop me fellowshipping with them, supporting and encouraging them, praying for them, exchanging insights from the Word with them - just because I myself have moved away from their traditions.

I wouldn't even try to draw them into our own new ways. No-one made any attempt to "convert" us. They told us of their own change, and left it at that, apart from answering any questions we asked. I believe that God has a big future for the "unstructured" churches, but it is He who will bring it about. If someone's inner convictions are leading in that direction, then I would want to encourage such a believer along the way. But I am not myself going to attempt to do the leading or to bring the conviction. **All I am trying to do in this book is to encourage dear friends in the unstructured churches that they are _well within God's framework_** in the way they are now moving; and to re-assure dear **friends in the "structured" churches that those of us who have "gone unstructured" have not gone off the rails as they may have feared.**

CHAPTER 6

BELIEVERS AT WORSHIP

In spite of what has already been argued, I'm sure that many of you, who are reading this, still have an uncomfortable niggle at the back of your minds with regard to these "unstructured" people and the Worship side of the Christian life. Though the Scriptures do not seem to carry a clear command for "regular corporate worship", the Bible is full of the more general command: "Worship the Lord your God". **And you are wondering how someone can be a satisfactory worshipper if he neglects such golden opportunities as Sunday services and meetings for worship!**

This question concerned me too in my early investigations of those who had "left the structures". But I felt I could only answer it if I had a definition, based on the Bible, of what worship actually is or of what makes a believer a "worshipper". So I went through the Bible, looking at every example of people worshipping. **To my surprise, I found that biblical references to worship taking place were, usually, quite unconnected with what you might call "religious meetings" or "services"!** IT BECAME CLEAR TO ME THAT WORSHIP WAS ALMOST ALWAYS A SPONTANEOUS EXPRESSION OF APPRECIATION TO THE LORD, FROM AMIDST WHATEVER SITUATIONS BELIEVERS FOUND THEMSELVES IN, RATHER THAN SOMETHING WHICH HAPPENED AT FIXED TIMES OR PLACES. Let me share with you some representative glimpses of believers at worship....

Remember the story of Abraham's servant looking for a wife for Isaac among the family's long-lost relatives? The first person he spoke to, on reaching his destination, turned out to be Isaac's lovely young second-cousin, Rebekah! Also, on a practical level, her father could offer the weary traveller accommodation for the night. The servant recognised all this as more than co-incidence. He appreciated that God was at work, and he expressed his appreciation. Here's how Genesis recounts it: "She answered him, 'I am the daughter of Bethuel, the son that Milcah bore to Nahor'. And she added, 'We have plenty of straw and fodder, as well as room for you to spend the night.' <u>Then the man bowed down and worshipped the Lord</u>, saying, 'Praise be to the Lord, the God of my master Abraham, who has not abandoned His kindness and faithfulness to my master. As for me, the Lord has led me on the journey to the house of my master's relatives.'" (Genesis 24:24-27). No service, no "worship time" - but worship!

Or consider a passage from Exodus. Moses had just returned to Egypt after his "burning bush" experience, with the call to lead the Israelites out of their slavery and oppression... "Moses and Aaron brought together all the elders of the Israelites, and

Aaron told them everything the Lord had said to Moses. He also performed the signs before the people, and they believed. And when they heard that the Lord was concerned about them and had seen their misery, they bowed down and worshipped." (Exodus 4:29-31)

Recall, for a moment, the incident when the not-very-confident Gideon was encouraged by the Lord to go down by night to the enemy camp, and listen to the conversations in the tents. He heard a soldier recounting a dream, which his mate interpreted as a run-away victory for Gideon! Judges 7:15 says: "When Gideon heard the dream and its interpretation, he worshipped God." It wasn't in a meeting. No service was arranged. It was "on-the-spot", spontaneous, in the course of life itself.

There is an unusual example of worship at the beginning of the book of Job. Job has just learned of a "freak" storm which has destroyed the house where all his family happened to be gathered together at the time. Each one of them had been killed. "At this, Job got up and tore his robe and shaved his head. Then he fell to the ground in worship, and said... 'The Lord gave, and the Lord has taken away: may the name of the Lord be praised'"(Job 1:20). I can understand why the Bible describes this tragic moment as "worship". In effect, Job was saying, by his actions and his words: "Lord, I am devastated by what has happened. But I know that Evil can't slip past You in the life of the believer. I appreciate the many years You gave me with my family, and I also appreciate that You would not have let this happen if it had not been within your good purposes." Worship from the heart, in a desperate situation.

In 1st and 2nd Chronicles, and even in the Psalms, there are, of course, some references to organised worship in the Temple. But we have to remember what was said earlier about the services in the Temple being limited - limited to those people who could travel regularly to the city of Jerusalem, and to those who lived in the years when there *was* a Temple. We also have to remember that Jesus told a woman, at the well in Samaria, that there would be no return to Jerusalem's Temple-worship - but that worship would, from then on, take place wherever people were moved in spirit to see God's true dealings with them (John 4:21,23).

As I worked through the Scriptures, it began to dawn on me that, on the whole, when someone was said to be worshipping it was usually outside "arrangements for worship". **Eventually I concluded that, *basically*, worship in the Old Testament was a spontaneous response of appreciation, when the good and wise dealings of the Lord were experienced or recalled. Worshippers of the Lord were those who consciously gave Him credit in their on-going situations**

I then discovered that the New Testament continues in exactly the same vein. It pictures the worshipper as someone who consciously expresses appreciation of the Lord on becoming aware of His handiwork. For example, after the incident when Peter tried to walk on the water during a storm, Jesus, also walking on the water, saved him from sinking. "And when they climbed into the boat, the wind died down. Then those who were in the boat worshipped Him, saying 'Truly, You are the Son of God'. (Matthew 14:32-33)

Or, remember the story, in John chapter 9, of the blind man whose eyes Jesus opened. In another sense, the man's eyes were later opened to the fact that Jesus was the Messiah. "Then the man said, 'Lord, I believe,' and he worshipped Him." (John 9:38)

This was also true of the women at the tomb on Easter Sunday morning: "Suddenly Jesus met them. 'Greetings', He said. They came to Him, clasped His feet, and worshipped Him." (Matthew 28:9). Like every one of the other incidents: there was no service, no worship-time - simply an expression, from the heart and mind, of appreciation and love.

I suspect that the reason the Epistles contain no command or urging to hold worship-services is that the first Christians already had this clear picture from Scripture of what was involved in being a worshipper.

Worship is a lifestyle. It is not, essentially, something you do at arranged times. It is based on a seven-days-a-week mind-set which acknowledges that the Lord is positively involved in everything. All Christians should be worshippers in the above Bible sense of the word. "Going to Church" does not make you a worshipper (though, as I shall say again in the next chapter, I don't for a moment deny that it *can* give you opportunities to worship, and might indeed stimulate and encourage your worship). But, by the same token "not-going-to-church" does not preclude you from being a worshipper. Mindset makes you a worshipper - not meetings!

*   *   *   *   *   *   *   *   *   *   *   *

Some people ask: "What about Communion, if you don't 'go to church'? Didn't Jesus give the command, talking of the bread and the wine, 'Do this in remembrance of me'?" This is probably as good a point as any to deal, very briefly, with these questions.

The impression I get from the Bible is that, just as worship was "in the course of life" in the early church, so was remembering the Lord's death with bread and wine. These were the staple food and drink of the first century Mediterranean world (and have remained so). I am by no means convinced that Jesus was commanding a "rite", a religious performance. That is not in keeping with Jesus at all. I believe He was simply saying that when believers shared a loaf of bread (the host would break it and distribute it - there was no sliced bread in those days) and when they shared wine together, they were to remember His broken body and poured out blood.

There are frequent New Testament references to "breaking bread" together in each other's homes. Sharing meals is still a feature of the life of Christian people, and such sharing is particularly highly valued among those of us who have moved away from set meeting places and regular organised meetings. The shared meal is a very authentic time and place to remember the Lord's death. This is not something new. I remember reading the biography of C.T. Studd, who was a famous English cricketer who became a missionary to China over a hundred years ago. This was the "way of communion" of him and his family. I believe it is very much in keeping with the intention of Jesus. What seems, to many Christians, to be the very "holy of holies" with regard to worship, is not absent outside the structures.

* * * * * * * * * * * *

All in all, when I consider the Christians whose church is not "normal" church, but a "house of living stones", I see them just as much as worshippers, of the kind we have been coming across in the pages of Scripture, as any other believers I know.

CHAPTER 7

SINGING TO THE LORD

I hope I have clarified the Bible's basic picture of believers at worship. It is relevant, however, to put alongside that picture a picture of believers singing. **The fact is that song, and togetherness-in-song, have an important part to play in the Christian life.**

The Psalms, (and many other parts of the Old Testament) often urge us to "Sing to the Lord". They also urge us to extend our repertoire from time to time! ("Sing a *new* song to the Lord".)

In the New Testament, the apostle Paul keeps up the urging for singing to be included in the Christian's lifestyle: "Let the word of Christ dwell in you richly, as you teach and admonish one another with all wisdom, and as you sing psalms, hymns and spiritual songs with gratitude in your hearts to God." (Colossians 3:16) The life of the Kingdom, as I see it in the Bible, is well interlaced with song!

Furthermore, it's quite clear that singing by believers is not to be confined to solo efforts! Believers are often to be found singing together in the pages of Scripture. I'm not talking about the singing in the Temple at Jerusalem, because that was usually done by a choir, and not by the congregation. There were, however, plenty of other occasions in the Old Testament when ordinary Jewish believers sang together to the Lord.

Here are some examples: when they had got safely over the Red Sea (Exodus 15:1); when they found a well of water springing up in the desert (Numbers 21:17); when they brought the Ark back to Jerusalem (1 Chronicles 13:8); when they returned from the "captivity" (Psalm 126:2); when they had rebuilt the walls of Jerusalem (Nehemiah 12:27). Admittedly, these were special occasions - but Old Testament believers must have built up a repertoire of songs they were accustomed to singing together, to be able to burst into community singing at these times of particular blessing!

It's just the same in the New Testament. We find Jesus and his disciples singing together as the "Last Supper" draws to a close (Matthew 26:30; Mark 14:26). In chapter 4 of this booklet, we have already observed hymn-singing at one of these occasional gatherings of the whole local church at Corinth (1 Corinthians 14:26). And, did you notice, when Paul was writing to the group in Colosse about the "psalms, hymns and spiritual songs", he was talking about a time when they would be *together*, building one another up in the faith (Colossians 3:16).

THERE IS A CLEAR LESSON IN ALL THIS FOR THOSE CHRISTIANS WHO ARE "OUTSIDE THE STRUCTURES". THEY MUST NOT LOSE TOUCH

WITH THE "SONGS OF ZION". THE MUSICAL HERITAGE OF THE PAST, TOGETHER WITH NEW SONGS AS THEY ARISE, IS THERE FOR THEM TO USE, PERSONALLY AND TOGETHER

* * * * * * * * * * *

They don't have to believe, however, that every time they sing psalms, hymns or spiritual songs, it must necessarily lead to worship, or to spiritual elation.

Many of these believers have come out of "charismatic" Fellowships where a time of Christian singing was thought to have "failed", if a certain atmosphere was not created. "I'm afraid that, today, we didn't get *through to Worship*" - that would be a typical remark you might hear from a disappointed Christian after an advertised "Worship-Time". There was an expectation that Christian singing-together should always lead to wonderful inner feelings or acute awareness of the Lord. This expectation, in turn, often seemed to be the cause of well-meaning but mis-guided attempts to contrive things and to manipulate people's responses.

That was not how it was in the Scriptures. As we saw earlier, real worship was something which "broke out" when there was a special realisation about God. It *could* happen during the singing of spiritual songs - but much more often it was at other times.

Nonetheless, the Bible still urges singing, and singing-together. That means that Christian singing-together should be valued for its own sake, whether or not it leads to worship or "atmosphere". As we sing, a response of worship *may* develop - but if it doesn't, that's quite acceptable.

In our own home, for instance, we get round the piano from time to time. (In other homes it would be round a guitar; a CD - or tape-player; or, perhaps most frequently, singing without any instrument.) We appreciate being able to "sing to the Lord". We accept that sometimes it's no more than singing - but sometimes our spirits are touched, and heartfelt worship is drawn from us.

Somehow, if Christians sing as individuals, or even as a family, there is no pressure to create Worship artificially. But if the numbers are larger, the pressure is on - especially if your background is the kind I've been describing. I have sometimes thought that, because of this danger, the Christians of the "loose associations" have been a bit over-cautious about "singing together".

But the danger of trying to contrive worship can easily be avoided by simply thinking in terms of "Let's sing together to the Lord" rather than having the more intense goal: "Let's have a time of Worship". As I said earlier, the Scriptures seem to value Christian singing-together for its own sake - quite apart from anything it might lead to. A straightforward mind-set of "Let's sing to the Lord" leaves room for worship to flow, if that is what is going to happen, but it doesn't create anything artificial.

* * * * * * * * * * * *

You should note, of course, that I am not at all saying that worship *cannot* flow from church-services and set "worship times". I freely admit that, over the years, we did experience some wonderful times of genuine worship during services and meetings - usually in the context of "singing to the Lord". There is no doubt at all that the "songs of Zion" can stimulate expressions of gratitude and appreciation to our Heavenly Father and to our Saviour. There is always the potential for that to happen whatever the setting - unstructured or structured. Indeed, the Bible gives an example of worship "breaking out" during singing (by the choir only!) in one of the "officially convened" Temple services. (Look up 2 Chronicles 29: 27-28 if you want details.)

So, my argument in this booklet is certainly not that worship cannot happen in pre-arranged worship services. What I am saying is that you don't have to have worship services in order to worship. Worship can flow out of down-to-earth "singing to the Lord", even when it is least expected. And worship can flow out of situations where singing is not involved at all!

You have to remember the message of the previous chapter - that the most usual stimulus to worship was a *realisation* about the Lord, and not a *song* about Him! Some of the most worshipful occasions I have known haven't had a note of music! Usually only small numbers of people were involved, sharing their experiences of God's good hand at work, not with cool matter-of-fact-ness, but with gratitude and wonder. I can think of some very special occasions when an unexpected coming-together of two couples, or of a few friends, led to a really powerful awareness of the Lord's presence, and an outpouring of worship to Him.

To sum up; I don't feel any need to criticise worship-services which other people find helpful. But I don't feel any need, either, to accept criticism myself because I don't "go to church". I happily accept the word of church-going- (or fellowship-going-) people when they say: "We had a wonderful time of worship", but I also affirm that the Christians "outside the structures" find their hearts drawn out in praise and worship in all kinds of situations, musical and non-musical.

A CAREFUL STUDY OF WHAT THE BIBLE ACTUALLY SAYS ABOUT WORSHIP HAS MADE IT ABUNDANTLY CLEAR TO ME THAT **THESE FOLK ARE *NOT* "MISSING OUT ON WORSHIP", EVEN THOUGH THEY DON'T ATTEND "WORSHIP SERVICES".**

* * * * * * * * * * *

But are they, perhaps, missing out on Teaching, or opportunities for "Outreach", or on proper Leadership? These issues are to be the subject of the third section of this booklet.

PART THREE

OTHER CHURCH ACTIVITIES FROM THE BIBLE'S VIEWPOINT

CHAPTER 8

TWO WORTHY WAYS OF TEACHING

I suspect that many Christians have never given a thought to Worship in the way I have described it in the previous two chapters. They have accepted unquestioningly the understanding of Worship which is current in the churches - namely, that it is something which really only happens at services and is particularly connected with singing. I hope I have shown that there is another way of looking at Worship which is perfectly valid in Scriptural terms.

The same is true about "Teaching" - the word the Bible uses for the instruction of Christians in matters of the Faith. The **approach to teaching generally accepted in the churches is not the *only* approach which is consistent with Scripture!**

I found that the instruction of believers, in the Bible record, was always done in one of two ways. Both ways were equally important - but there were times when the first way was the appropriate one to use, and other times when the second way was more suitable. I am going to take the whole of this chapter to examine these two ways as we find them in Scripture, because I believe that, in church circles, one of the ways has been greatly over-emphasised at the expense of the other. I am going to go on to suggest that the folks outside the structures are merely redressing the balance.

* * * * * * * * * * * *

The first of the two ways-of-teaching which we find in the Bible is what I would call LECTURE TEACHING; but then there is also what might be termed COMMENTS-IN-THE-COURSE-OF-LIFE TEACHING. Let us look at each of these in turn...

By "Lecture Teaching" I mean any kind of continuous talk by one speaker, almost always without interruption; the kind of thing that, nowadays, we would call "a sermon" or "preaching" or "an address" or even "a talk" or "a word" or "sharing", etc., etc.

"Lecture Teaching" for believers has an honourable place all through the Scriptures. Deuteronomy Chapter 5 begins like this: "Moses summoned all Israel and said...." From that point on, right up to the end of chapter 30, the text seems to be one long lecture or sermon. It begins with the giving of the Ten Commandments, and the rest of it is a filling out of the detailed implications of the Commandments.

Another famous lecture session was when the Exiles had returned to Jerusalem in the time of Nehemiah the Governor, and Ezra the Priest. A generation had grown up which was pretty ignorant of the Laws of Moses. So, "All the people assembled in the square before the Water-Gate, Ezra brought the Law before the assembly... and read it aloud from daybreak till noon. The Levites (thirteen of them) instructed the people... They read from the book of the Law of God, making it clear, and giving the meaning, so that the people could understand what was being read." (Nehemiah 8:1-3,7-8) This was definitely "lecture teaching".

Jesus is reported as sometimes teaching by the lecture method. John's Gospel chapters 15 and 16 seem to be an un-interrupted, continuous talk; and everyone is familiar, of course, with the "Sermon on the Mount". There's also what you might call the "Sermon from the Boat" when Jesus taught from a "pulpit" in the form of a boat a little distance from the shore (Luke 5:3) - though there is no account of what was actually said on that occasion.

The Apostles within the early church certainly gave fairly long talks or "sermons" to the general public in outdoor situations. These normally followed some unusual happening or miracle. They started off as a comment on what had happened, because there was a ready audience looking for an explanation. Such "sermons" usually resulted in some of the hearers becoming believers. However, these "sermons" are not particularly relevant to the subject of the instruction of those who are already believers, which is what we're talking about in this chapter.

Nevertheless, the "lecture-method" *was* used for teaching those who were already Christians. In Acts 20:18-35, Paul speaks to the Christian elders in Ephesus in a short address - a "lecture" in itself. In the course of his address (verse 20), he refers to having taught the believers there "publicly" - which does give the impression that something like teaching-by-sermons had been taking place.

Earlier on in that same chapter was the all-night sermon which Paul gave to the Christian group in the ancient city of Troy: "Paul spoke to the people and, because he intended to leave the next day, kept on talking till midnight... Paul talked on and on... After talking till daylight, he left." (Acts 20:7,9,11). We probably couldn't take too much of that kind of "lecture teaching", but nonetheless, it does remind us that lecture teaching was a part of New Testament church life.

* * * * * * * * * * *

However, just as important in both New and Old Testaments - just as prominent as a way of instructing believers - was what I have already termed "*Comment-in-the-course-of-life Teaching*". Let me illustrate from Scripture. Moses had hardly begun his "Ten Commandments Sermon" than he was explaining how these important guidelines should be taught in future: "These commandments that I give you today are to be on your hearts. Impress them on your children. **Talk about them when you sit at home and when you walk along the road, when you lie down and when you get up.** (Deuteronomy 6:6-7, repeated in chapter 11:19) Surely this is "comment in the course of life"!

Now, I don't personally think that this key verse applies exclusively to children. A method was being suggested for impressing God's requirements on children *and* for keeping His commands in the hearts of adults. But certainly, so far as children-within-the-family-of-God are concerned, there is further evidence of this method being used in Old Testament times. Moses goes on to suggest that children will ask "spiritual" questions, which should be answered out of the parents' own experience (Deuteronomy 6:20-25). The Book of Proverbs gives the distinct impression that the young Jew of the day received his instruction, not by being lectured by a Priest or Levite, but from the comments of his Dad and Mum! Verses like "When I was a boy in my father's house....he taught me" (Proverbs 4:3,4) or "Do not forsake your mother's teaching" (Proverbs 1:8) sum up the whole ethos of the book.

There is no evidence of the first method of teaching we considered ("lecture teaching") before the giving of the Ten Commandments. So I don't think it is unfair to suggest that the earliest "heroes of the faith", such as Noah, Abraham, Joseph and the young Moses, probably received their grasp of spiritual truth through this second method - the "Comments" method. They were almost certainly taught by their parents and elders, within the believing community, as situations arose.

Turning from the practice of the Jews to the practice of the first Christians, we find that the Acts of the Apostles mentions "Comments-Teaching" just as much as "Lecture-Teaching". Here are a few examples (I could go on and on about it):

When Peter returned to Jerusalem after one of his trips, some of the Christians there found fault with him because they had heard that he had "eaten with Gentiles". So Peter simply recounted his experiences, and especially God's supernatural intervention in the matter, and, as a result, the whole Church learned that the barriers between Jew and Gentile had been broken down. (Acts 11:1-18). It wasn't a sermon or a lecture: it was merely a question of comments made as a situation arose.

In Acts 18:24-25 we see Apollos teaching, in sermon form, in a synagogue. (This was in the early days before the Christians stopped operating through the synagogues.) But in the very next verse we see him in quite a different teaching situation. This time he is in a simple threesome in the home of a married couple; and this time, in fact, he is on the receiving end of the instruction! No sermon was involved - only conversation which had been stimulated by happenings earlier in the day. And yet, teaching was taking place.

In Acts 19:1-7, Paul comes across a dozen "disciples" and gets the distinct impression that they don't have the experience of the Holy Spirit which he had come to expect. By question and answer he gets to the root of the problem, and shows them the way forward, which they gladly respond to. There's no evidence of a "sermon approach". Again, "comments-in-the-course-of-life teaching" is what is taking place.

There are various references in the Epistles to everyone teaching everyone else. It seems unlikely, in these cases, that "teaching" equals "delivering a sermon"! It seems much more realistic to imagine people instructing each other in the course of conversation. "Let the word of Christ dwell in you richly as you teach and admonish one another with all wisdom" (Colossians 3:16). That certainly suggests believers should be drawing on their knowledge of the teachings of Jesus to educate each other in Christian ways - but it carries no hint that they should be addressing their fellow-believers in sermon form! Similarly, when the writer to the Hebrews writes to a *general* audience: "By this time you ought to be teachers" (Heb.5:12) he can hardly be meaning that all Christians should eventually be able to give a sermon!

The most telling New Testament point of all, however, is, that Jesus mainly used the "comments-in-the-course-of-life" method of teaching. Although, as I have already acknowledged, an occasional "sermon" by Jesus is reported, a very large proportion of the Gospel record consists in *incidents and conversations during which Jesus gave explanations or instructions*. Go through Matthew, Mark, Luke and John for yourself, page by page, and you will see that there is much much more "Commenting" than there is "Sermonising" or "Lecturing".

* * * * * * * * * * *

MY EXPERIENCE OF THE "UNSTRUCTURED CHURCHES" IS THAT THEY ARE COMMITTED TO THE BIBLE'S "COMMENTS-IN-THE-COURSE-OF-LIFE TEACHING", (THE METHOD MOST FREQUENTLY USED BY JESUS) - WITHOUT NEGLECTING THE PLACE GIVEN IN SCRIPTURE TO "LECTURE TEACHING". But I shall leave it to the next chapter to elaborate on that assertion.

CHAPTER 9

PRACTICALITIES OF TEACHING
- THEN AND NOW

These new "loose associations" of Christians - houses of living stones - seem to me to use "Comments-in-the-Course-of-Life Teaching" quite effectively.

One of the things which has surprised and impressed me most about the believers outside the structures, is the Christian upbringing of their **children.** Of course, it's only fair to admit that my observations are based on a limited number of families. (In fact, the whole "unstructured church" is very limited in numbers, as yet.) But even a few examples show me what the possibilities are. Children whose parents have been outside the structures for half-a-dozen years or more, seem just as full of Christian awareness, and just as well instructed, as those who have come up through the "normal" system. Furthermore, parents in the institutional churches can be tempted to leave a lot to "Sunday School" or to youth groups, or even to the children's presence at the predominantly adult Sunday service or meeting. But the parents in the loose associations know that Christian nurture is definitely **their** responsibility! I've seen enough to convince me that Comments-in-the-Course-of-Life Teaching has very great potential in the teaching of children within Christian families. (In case you're wondering about "reaching out" to children who don't come from Christian families, I've written something about that later.)

I have also had a glimpse of the "Comments" method, with regard to the instruction of individual **new converts.** I've seen real progress made, even in a scene where there are no sermons and no weekly nurture-groups-with-a-teaching-talk. Of course, there has to be one-to-one commitment on someone's part; someone who is willing to "disciple" the new believer. Given that, it is clear to me that a "young Christian" **can** be very well taught by the "Commments-in-the-Course-of-Life" method.

So far as believers who already have a reasonable "grounding" in the basics of the Faith are concerned, teaching by the "Comments" method seems to me to be highly effective. I suspect this is because it is what I might call "TAILORED TEACHING". Comments-instruction is "made to measure"! It deals with people's actual situations; with the actual questions they are asking; and with actual gaps in their understanding of God and His ways. It is specific to the issues in people's lives. In the "houses of living stones", believers give teaching to each other *where it is required,* either because someone has shared an area of need with them, or because they themselves have sensed that something could usefully be said.

I hope I'm making myself clear. I'm back to the kind of situation I mentioned in the very first chapter, where those teachers in the High School who were committed Christians, were such a help to each other - not least in applying the Word of God where it was needed. This is exactly the kind of teaching I find in the "loose associations", for which my school experience was a parable. It doesn't even need a "gathering" to take place - though it can, of course, happen when a fair number of these Christians in the locality have met together. But, just as this kind of informal teaching took place in such places as the school's Staff Room, or the school corridors, or in casual evening socialising, - so, in the wider scene, it can happen during a "chance" encounter in the street, or shopping centre, or workplace; on a visit to someone's home; over the telephone or in a letter. (These last two are particularly important to the scattered outside-the-structures Christians who live in rural areas.) Whatever the point of contact, appropriate teaching seems to take place.

Of course, sometimes someone would share something he or she had discovered, without any reference to particular situations - a discovery which seemed to them to be a kind of "gem of truth"; something which had been noticed in personal Bible reading, or in some other way. Even though it wasn't directed to anyone or any situation in particular, it had a vitality about it, because it sprang from someone's enthusiastic response to what they had come across. They didn't *have* to share it, but they did so because they were excited about it. Truth is truth - but there is "dull" truth and there is "fresh" truth.

I've heard some great sermons and talks over the years, but sometimes sermons and talks have a dullness about them because something *must* be said on that occasion. It is 11.45 on a Sunday morning, and everyone expects it - but it may not speak into real situations, nor flow from a fresh discovery on the part of the speaker. I am convinced that churches of all types, from the denominations with their roots deep in History to the newest charismatic fellowships, have *over stressed* the importance of sermons, addresses and talks (everything I have called "Lecture Teaching"). Many of the folks I know "outside the structures" are mature and "teachable" Christians who are finding the Bible's honoured method of "Comments-in-the-Course-of-Life Teaching" very refreshing indeed.

*   *   *   *   *   *   *   *   *   *

At this point it would be very fair for you to ask me "How do you get a right balance then? If the 'normal' churches have gone overboard with sermons and talks, are these new 'loose associations' not going to the other extreme, and throwing out 'Lecture Teaching' altogether - even though you say that it, also, has an honourable a place in the Scriptures?" In answer to that question, I would ask you to look at the Bible to see **when** Lecture-Teaching is used. LECTURE-TEACHING IS USED, ACCORDING TO THE RECORD OF SCRIPTURE, WHEN A FAIR AMOUNT OF **NEW** MATERIAL HAS TO BE IMPARTED TO QUITE A LARGE GROUP OF PEOPLE. This can either mean that there are, all at once, a great many new Christians who know absolutely nothing, and need a good grounding, or it can mean that there is a biggish group of Christians who already have a basic grounding, but something new has been revealed, which they need to learn about. Let's look at some examples, first of all from the book of Acts.

Acts 11:19-21, for instance, explains that a "great number" of non-Jews in the city of Antioch turned to the Lord. Suddenly, there was a big crowd of people, all at the same stage - totally ignorant Christians who didn't even know the Old Testament! Barnabas was sent to suss out the situation, and he thought it a good idea to involve Paul (then still using his old name of "Saul"): "For a whole year Saul and Barnabas met with the church and taught great numbers of people." (verse 26, but see from 22 on). **It definitely sounds like "lecture-teaching" (sermons, addresses) - and it looks as though that was the normal way of dealing with converts when there were too many for realistic one-to-one discipling.**

Paul and Barnabas obviously gave the believers in Antioch a good grounding during their year's stay there. After that, they went on some fairly extensive travels, recounted in Acts chapters 13 and 14. When they next visited Antioch, they found that a new issue had arisen: Did all these non-Jews who had become Christians need to go through the Jewish rite of circumcision? Quite a number of the local Christians were very bothered about this matter, and **it became clear that the whole group *now* needed teaching about how - if at all - the old Jewish practices fitted in.** After a consultation with other apostles and elders at Jerusalem, Paul and Barnabas, (accompanied by Silas and one other leader) held a new "lecture" session with all the believers gathered together. You can read all about it in Acts 15, especially verses 30-35. **It was a case of new "lecturing" for new material.**

Very similar, in the Old Testament, was Moses' "lecture" or sermon at the foot of Mount Sinai (which takes up most of the book of Deuteronomy). The listeners, in spite of all their faults, were already God's People. They weren't "new converts". But God had something new to impart to all of them at this particular juncture. Because they had not proved to be very good at walking in personal relationship with Him, God wanted His People, for a period at least, to have the unmistakable guidelines of The Law. Once again, it was a case of "new lecturing for new material", with a large group of people all starting from scratch.

(An aside here: Towards the end of his sermon, Moses said, in effect, "We must do this again sometime". But his suggestion was not, as it might be in the modern church, to do it again in seven days time - but to do it again in seven years time! (Deut. 31:9-13))

Another Old Testament example of "Lecture-Teaching" is to be found in 2 Chronicles chapter 17. The godless King Asa had reigned for forty-one years, during which time the nation of Judah had gone into serious spiritual decline. Then along comes Asa's son Jehoshaphat who "walked in the ways which his ancestor David had followed". "In the third year of his reign he sent his officials... to teach in the towns of Judah. With them were certain Levites. They taught throughout Judah, taking with them the Book of the Law of the Lord; they went round all the towns of Judah and taught the people" (2 Chron. 17:7-9). Once again, people were not complete newcomers to the faith - but very much in need of a refresher course. And because there were quite a few believers at the same stage, "Lecture Teaching" was the appropriate way of giving it.

Teaching *in that way* did not, however, continue indefinitely. Once people had received a grounding, or a re-grounding, these "Travelling Teachers" or "Old Testament Apostles" departed, and there is no evidence of any further lecture-teaching being undertaken in the districts they had left. On the other hand, as we have seen, Comments-in-the-course-of-Life Teaching" was a genuine feature of Old Testament life, and is likely to have been the follow-up to their visit.

This is exactly the pattern we see in the New Testament. The Apostles (the "Travelling Teachers" of the New Testament) gave their teaching-sermons or teaching-addresses (to be distinguished from their preaching-sermons, which were "evangelistic") either to groups of new believers, or to groups of established believers who were all in need of a new area of instruction. Then they went away and left any further teaching for believers to their fellow-Christians and to their leaders (more about "elders" and "pastors-and-teachers" in a later chapter). But there is no mention of lecture-teaching being done by anyone other than the "Travelling Teachers" or Apostles. On the other hand, as we have already seen, there are plenty of references to "Comments-Teaching" in the on-going New Testament Church.

* * * * * * * * * *

What I have been describing is very much how things are, among the believers outside the structures"! By not attending at regular sermons or talks, they are not saying that these are wrong, but only that their frequent use is a Custom which has developed, but not a Command of Scripture. The *command* is to be teachable and to go on learning - but these "outsiders" *are* doing that.

Most of them have "grounding" and some maturity. So "Comments-in-the-Course-of-Life", from fellow-believers, and from those who emerge as leaders, is the normal and appropriate way of teaching. There are some "Travelling Teachers" among them, who, like Paul in Acts 20:20, seem to teach "publicly and from house to house" - "publicly", when there is some new insight to be shared with everyone; but visiting believers in their own homes, so that there can be "made-to-measure" teaching also. "New converts" can be handled by one-to-one discipling. If, however, a large number of "raw recruits" appears all at once, there is no rule among these particular Christians that talks and addresses cannot be used!

ALL THINGS CONSIDERED, TEACHING "OUTSIDE THE STRUCTURES" SEEMS, TO ME, TO KEEP IN STEP WITH BIBLE WAYS OF DOING THINGS.

CHAPTER 10

THE TASK WHICH FOLLOWS THE TEACHING

In everyday life, people expect that your education will be followed by a job. In one sense, of course, you should go on learning all through your life; but INTENSIVE teaching should be at the early stages. There may be refresher courses from time to time - but mainly it will be "in-service training", topping up as the need arises. Initially, you concentrate on being instructed, but after that (though you always remain open to further teaching) you concentrate on the task before you each day.

This seems to have been the way that the first Apostles operated. They saw to it that their converts got intensive instruction at the beginning of their Christian lives, but then they themselves moved on, expecting the believers to become PREOCCUPIED WITH THE JOB CHRISTIANS ARE SUPPOSED TO UNDERTAKE. Let Paul and Peter, in particular, explain in some detail what they considered that job to be:

"We are...created in Christ Jesus to do good works" (Ephesians 2:10). "Each one should use whatever gift he has received to serve others, faithfully administering God's grace in its various forms" (1 Peter 4:10). "Each of you should please his neighbour for his good, to build him up" (Romans 15:2). This job-Christians-are-supposed-to-undertake can be summed up in a few key phrases from these verses: **to do good works; to serve others... neighbours... in... various forms.** The Task, in other words, is to bless (i.e. to benefit) other people, in every way they might need blessing, - physically, practically, socially, mentally, spiritually - just the kind of thing which Jesus Himself did in His lifetime, and taught others to do.

The "Apostles' Teaching" laid this message on quite thickly, especially Peter's point about being ready to share God's grace across the whole spectrum of ways it might be needed. "We pray this: that you might live a life worthy of the Lord, and may please Him <u>in every way</u>, bearing fruit in every good work" (Colossians 1:10). "If a man cleanses himself... he will be an instrument for noble purposes... useful to the Master, and prepared to do <u>any</u> good work" (2 Timothy 2:21). "Well known for her good deeds such as...showing hospitality, helping those in trouble, and devoting herself to <u>all kinds of good deeds</u>. (1 Timothy 5:10). Both Peter and Paul remind believers that there is a "spiritual" dimension to good deeds: "Always be prepared to give an answer to everyone who asks you, ...for the hope that you have" (1 Peter 3:15). "...Shine like stars in the universe, <u>as you hold out the word of life</u>" (Philippians 2:15,16).

Moving on from Peter and Paul, don't forget James's key phrase: "Faith without Deeds is dead" (James 2:26 - and see also verses 14, 17 and 20 of the same chapter). Remember, too, why the writer to the Hebrews said we should 'assemble ourselves together': "Let us consider how we may <u>spur one another on towards love and good deeds</u>" (Heb 10:24)

Paul makes the point that a **major** purpose of TEACHING, and, in one sense, of Scripture itself, is to prepare believers for the TASK OF BLESSING OTHERS: "All scripture is God-breathed and is useful for teaching, rebuking, correcting and training in righteousness, <u>so that the man of God may be thoroughly equipped for every good work</u>" (2 Tim. 3:16,17) Elsewhere Paul had said, like Jesus before him: "The entire Law is summed up in a single command, 'Love your neighbour as yourself' "(Gal 5:14).

I have by no means exhausted the scriptures relating to this particular issue, but I hope enough has been said to show that the Apostles took THE TASK WHICH FOLLOWS THE TEACHING very seriously.

* * * * * * * * * *

It was quite rare, in the New Testament Church, for this task, this "blessing of others", to be **organised,** or to involve a big number of people working together on a project. Where there are reports, in the pages of Scripture, of the above teaching being put into operation, it is being done by ones and twos, as opportunities, or situations of need, arose. Read through the Acts, and you will come across account after account of the spontaneous work of individuals or of pairs: Peter and John (ch.3), Barnabas, and many other individuals (ch.4), Gamaliel (ch.5), Stephen (ch.6,7), Philip (ch.8), Ananias (ch.9), Peter again (ch. 10-12), Barnabas and Paul (ch 13)..and so it goes on. You will notice that the people involved are both apostles *and* "ordinary Christians". If you do read through Acts, you will also notice that, with very very few exceptions, there was nothing organised, individually or "corporately".

There were, of course, odd occasions in the story of the New Testament Church, when organisation at the human level *was* involved. One such appears in Acts 6 (1-7) where seven men were chosen to take over responsibility for the daily distribution of food to needy widows. (By this time the Church in Jerusalem had grown to 5000 people at the very least - see Acts 4:4 - yet this is the only bit of organisation reported from there!) Another example is Paul's organising all the local churches of south-eastern Europe to collect donations for the poverty-stricken Jerusalem Christians (1 Corinthians 16:1-4 and Romans 15:25-27 tell the story).

Generally speaking, however, there is very little evidence of much organisation being involved in the carrying out of "the Task". Usually it was left to individuals noticing opportunities, or being prompted by the Holy Spirit to know what the needs were. We might be tempted to think that these individual efforts would be rather a hit-and-miss affair, but the Holy Spirit seems to have co-ordinated everyone's efforts most effectively!

The fact is that, even without much organisation, and with the

very minimum of projects or schemes, they were *highly successful* in blessing others. Many people were converted; many were healed physically, and delivered from oppression; and practical needs were catered for - so well, in some situations, that the Christians earned great public respect. (e.g. "They gave to anyone as he had need....enjoying the favour of all the people" - Acts 2:45,47).

* * * * * * * * * *

Let me sum up what has been said, so far, in this chapter. The first Christians, if they had listened to the "Apostle's Teaching", knew exactly what their purpose in life was; as each new day dawned, they would have had a clear vision of their reason for living. **It was to bless other people, for Jesus' sake.** (Christians today should still have this clear daily vision.) The Early Church was made to understand that they were to do it in a wide variety of ways, ranging from down-to-earth practical care, right through to being "fishers of men", helping others to come into the Kingdom.

There is no evidence of them finding problems with *how* to do this. They seem to have relied on the Holy Spirit to give them opportunities, or "channels of service", among the people they came across quite naturally. Very rarely indeed did they actually organise "channels of service" for themselves (though some of them did move from place to place to find new opportunities). They were simply dedicated to living for others, in the neighbourhood, in the workplace, at home, at leisure, in socialising, wherever. That was, for them, "Christian Work" and "Outreach into the Community". There is very little sign of either "regular meetings" or "special events" - indeed of anything resembling the Church Programmes of today. **It was service-in-the-course-of-everyday-life, and, certainly in those days, it was highly effective.**

I SINCERELY BELIEVE THAT THOSE WHO HAVE "LEFT THE STRUCTURES" ARE TRYING TO GET BACK TO THAT TASK - THAT SIMPLE, YET BIBLICAL, STYLE OF CHRISTIAN SERVICE.

Is that realistic in modern times? Is there any hope of their ways being effective? Is nothing *ever* to be organised? These are questions we shall deal with in the next two chapters....

CHAPTER 11

DOES 'INFORMAL' = 'INEFFECTIVE'?

I have to admit right away that the style of Christian Service adopted by those whose only church is a "house of living stones" is not nearly so "reportable" as the usual church activities - certainly not in the short term at any rate. Simply to be relating to people, and being there for them (though very time-consuming, and potentially very valuable) doesn't give you much to report to other Christians - unless, of course, it happens to involve some kind of specific activity.

You could, for instance, give a great deal of much-needed time to Joe Bloggs, or the whole Bloggs family - time which, in the long run, might benefit them greatly in various areas of life; might even lead to someone's conversion to Christ. But unless you regularly engage in some special outing or event with them (which you will probably do occasionally, of course) your actual week-by-week, month-by-month "Christian Service" could well sound rather boring! Even if you were in touch with scores of people, one way and another, in the course of a year, it still wouldn't make much of an "Annual-Newsletter" - except when, from time to time, a whole jigsaw of influences on someone's life comes together, or God breaks in, in a supernatural way. The fact is that, generally speaking, if you want fellow-Christians to feel that you are doing something vital for the Lord, it is certainly easier to be able to tell about meetings and missions, planning-sessions and projects.

However, don't let that blind you to the fact that ultra-informal ways of "outreach into the community" have proved very effective, even in the 20th Century - just as they did in the First Century.

One of the most amazing books I have read in recent years is "Bruchko" - an autobiography by an American, Bruce Olson. I believe it is very relevant to what I'm trying to say. As a young man Olson went as a missionary to Colombia. Circumstances separated him from the other missionaries he had originally come to join, and he found himself alone, deep in the jungle, living among the Motilones - a murderous tribe of stone-age people. Traditional missionary methods proved of absolutely no avail, and for years he had to content himself with simply being a contributing member of the community. He engaged in the same necessary work as everyone else, but he also tried to introduce better agricultural techniques and healthier ways of doing things, without in any way destroying their unique culture. Life was very harsh, and it is difficult to imagine how he could have lasted the pace, had God not intervened supernaturally to heal him and to help him.

The years passed. Occasionally "Bruchko" (i.e. Bruce - as pronounced by the Indians) had opportunities, in the course of conversation, to explain some of the things he believed - but nobody acted on what he said about Christ. Then one day Bobarishora, his closest friend among the tribesmen, following yet another conversation on the deepest things of life, told him that he had "tied his hammock strings into Jesus". It was clear as they talked further that the tribesman had genuinely turned to the Lord. Bruchko was very excited. "I wanted him to call a meeting and tell the rest about Jesus... He could do it more effectively than I... I wanted him to do it the way things would have been done in North America... I wanted to squeeze him into the mould."

But Bobarishora (Bruce nicknamed him Bobby) would have none of it! He couldn't set up something which the rest of the community would recognise as artificial. He did admit in conversation that he had become a Christian, but he wouldn't hold any meetings or do anything publicly. Time passed. "Bobby" married and became one of the respected younger leaders among the tribesmen. Then one day an older chief invited him to take part in the traditional "Festival of Arrows", which meant singing a Saga-Song to everyone. Bruchko writes: "Bobby's song was about the way the Motilones had been deceived and had lost God's trail. Then he began to sing about Jesus... Everyone became quiet in order to listen. The song continued for ten hours (!!!)...That night a spiritual revolution swept over the people. No one rejected the news about Jesus. Everyone wanted Him.. There was tremendous jubilation. God had spoken... He had spoken through the Motilone culture". After that there was great progress - such progress that Bruce Olsen has several times been asked to address the United Nations on how it was that helpful methods of hygiene and farming, *and Christianity,* were introduced into a primitive culture, without effacing that culture, or turning it into a pale reflection of the United States! HE DID SEE FRUIT FOR HIS 'INFORMAL' LABOURS - IN THE LONG RUN.

I know this is an outstanding and exceptional story, but the principle behind it is the principle I have been trying to explain. **If, as a Christian, you have a heart and mind to bless other people, and an openness to needs and opportunities around you, God will co-ordinate your actions with the contributions of others, and bring about much blessing in His own good time. There will be no need to contrive artificial "channels" for reaching out to others - evangelistically, or for any other form of Christian service.**

As I have already said several times, that was the experience of the first Christians. It has also been the experience of the Chinese Church in the 20th Century. According to reports from numerous sources, quite independent of each other, the number of active Christians in China grew phenomenally in the years when no church activities were permitted! (Incidentally, I find it intriguing that the famous Christian author, Watchman Nee, became an advocate of "unstructured churches" in the late 1930s.)

Of course, you could point out that these situations were all different from "Western" society today. In the situations I have been talking about, church activities were either inappropriate or else they were banned altogether. You may feel that where church activities are permitted, and show some signs of success, they should be engaged in wholeheartedly. That's fair enough, provided you don't dismiss those "outside the structures" as ineffective or heretical. **In point of fact, they are standing in a very definite biblical tradition, with regard to how they go about the "Task" of being concerned for others.**

Once again, it's a question of "Custom and Command". The Command is: to love and serve others in every area of human need. I see no need to criticise how you, using your church activities and organisations, carry out that command -your Customs of Service. By the same token, I think it is out of place for you to criticise the methods of service of those of us who have "gone unstructured". We have asked ourselves a question all Christians should ask about what they are doing: "Is this in line with scripture?". We believe the answer is a very definite "Yes". We have also asked ourselves another question (even though you don't really need to ask this one, if you are sure God is calling you to something): "Have we any evidence that our methods have any chance of success?". Once again, the answer is a resounding "Yes"...

"Each one of you should use whatever gift he has to serve others, faithfully administering God's grace in its various forms" (1Peter 4:10). *That* is Christian Service, and CHRISTIAN SERVICE IS ALIVE AND WELL AMONG THOSE OUTSIDE THE STRUCTURES IN THE "HOUSES OF LIVING STONES".

CHAPTER 12

KEEPING ORGANISATION IN ITS PROPER PLACE

Am I suggesting that "unstructured" Christians should have nothing whatever to do with anything organised? Not at all! I believe first of all that, in practical matters, it is vital to organise things properly. I even believe that, under certain circumstances, organisations can have a place within the informal lifestyle-of-service I have been talking about. But Christians have to know how to keep this human tendency - to organise everything - firmly in its place. Otherwise it can get very out-of-hand! We have already seen that there was organising in the New Testament - when order needed to be brought to a practical situation (the distribution of food to the needy widows in Acts 6).

For my own part, I have never seen anything very "spiritual" about leaving the Holy Spirit to attend to the carrying-out of practical matters! I well remember, from my early days of Christian service, some very zealous folks who showed excellent cinema-style films to young people (in the days before videos were available) - but they never had the correct electrical plugs, or a properly maintained projector, and they often forgot to check if a hall could be adequately darkened! They couldn't understand why there were so many disasters, when they were "trusting the Holy Spirit"! They had forgotten that His role is to initiate, direct and empower, but not to make all the actual arrangements.

So, if the Spirit inspires you, say, to take a difficult teenager on an outing or a holiday; and gives you the abundant grace and wisdom you will certainly need; please be prepared, at least, to do the booking, and make a list of things to take, and investigate possible pastimes for when you're there, and generally get organised - yourself! This principle applies in many situations. God forbid that a breed of Christian emerges which leaves practical arrangements in chaos, out of some false sense of spirituality. Happily, I haven't seen any sign of this attitude developing among the folks I've been talking about.

* * * * * * * * * *

As well as commending the sensible organising-of-arrangements when that became necessary, the New Testament also had a **small** place for organisations. Paul's project for helping the famine victims in Jerusalem (mentioned on several occasions in the New Testament) was a kind of organisation, set up when a clear call from God could only be accomplished by involving Christians from widely scattered local churches.

I have noticed, from time to time, that the Christians of the "loose associations" (as I called them in chapter 2) *are* associated with such organisations. Let me give you a personal example. Like many other Christians, Mavis and I contribute to a scheme which sponsors children in the "Third World". I think it's a great "organisation", and I'm sure it touches an area of need which would not otherwise be touched. In fact, I am full of admiration for quite a number of schemes and projects I have observed, or read about, or been involved with, over the years, usually in areas of extreme human need.

*   *   *   *   *   *   *   *   *   *

Unfortunately, however, Christians have a tendency to organise everything. It sometimes seems as if they can only think of the service-of-others in organisational terms. Whenever there is a need - a practical need, a social need, an evangelistic need - it seems to be assumed, nowadays, that it can only be met by some kind of organisation. There has not been anything like the same emphasis on Christians being constantly alive to such needs in the course of everyday life.

But the setting-up of organisations can very easily become counter-productive. There are two reasons for this. The first is that Christians can become so embroiled in a welter of church activities that there is no time left for REAL CONTACT WITH REAL PEOPLE - even though the activities were originally designed to help Christians be a blessing to others. A believer is often considered to be "very committed" if he is involved in numerous activities - whereas that very involvement can seriously undermine the real commitment of "being where Jesus is" - alongside those in need. Often I have heard those who have come out of "structured" church-life saying "Isn't it wonderful to have time and flexibility to do the things you sense the Lord is really calling you to?" Of course, ditching organisations could be a "cop-out" for lazy Christians who don't want to do anything, but for those who have caught the simple vision of being-available-for-Jesus-and-for-Others, the new freedom is very welcome and creative.

The second counter-productive element is this: **organisation can very easily take the "personal touch" out of Love.** In my young days, children "in care" used to be looked after in institutions like Orphanages and Children's Homes. I have no doubt that much good work was done. But nowadays the emphasis is rightly on Fostering and Adoption - taking the care of such young people out of the sphere of institutions-and-organisations, and into the normal course of life. I believe quite strongly that this principle should apply to "Church Work". People are much more blessed by getting sincere personal attention, than by being on the receiving end of some project. Furthermore, it's easier for Christians to "weary in well-doing" where a project is concerned, than where a genuine friendship has been built up.

Someone once suggested that those outside the structures had no possibility of "reaching" (in the evangelistic sense) children and young people who are not in Christian families. But many "unstructured Christians" are in touch with children and young people in the normal course of events - through their own families, or jobs, or neighbourhoods. Whenever Christians are in touch with others, there is the potential for blessing others every way Jesus commends - including encouraging them through to discipleship. "Results" might be *slower* than with Organisations, but I suspect they might also be *surer*. Among children and young people reached by organisational projects, there is a huge fall-out rate.

However, I am straying into the area of criticising other people's customs of Service. So far as possible, I am determined not to do this. **The New Testament is full of commands not to criticise fellow Christians.** In Romans 14 (vv4,13) Paul writes: "Who are you to judge someone else's servant? To his own Master he stands or falls... Let us stop passing judgment on one another." In 1 Corinthians 11 (v 31) he warns: "If we judged ourselves, we would not come under judgement". He was following the line taken by Jesus Himself: "When Peter saw John, he asked 'Lord, what about him?' Jesus answered: 'If I want him to (follow a certain course of action), what is that to you? As for you, see to it that you follow me'" (John 21:21,22 - attempting to catch the emphases of the original Greek). So, we are to judge our own ways of doing things, but not other people's! This may sometimes mean asking "Am I to do it the way they do it?", - but the follower of Christ ought to be keeping clear of finding fault with fellow believers.

ALL I WANT TO EMPHASISE IS: SERVICE-WITHOUT-ORGANISATIONS, **SERVICE-IN-THE-COURSE-OF-LIFE, IS BIBLICAL AND REALISTIC.**

CHAPTER 13

LEADERSHIP IS LOW-KEY, BUT LIBERATING

You must have noticed that, in the scenario which I have been describing, there has been hardly any mention, so far, of local **leadership.** It wouldn't surprise me if you are asking: "Do they have any leaders in these "houses of living stones" - and, if they have, what on earth do these leaders actually do?"

I would like to answer these questions by looking at some of the references to local leadership in the New Testament. You will soon begin to realise that LOCAL LEADERSHIP WAS VERY LOW-KEY, and you will also begin to see what exactly it involved.

Commenting on leadership among the "Gentiles", Jesus once said (Mark 10:42-44): "You know that... their high officials exercise authority over them. Not so with you. Instead, whoever wants to become great among you must be your servant, and whoever wants to be first must be slave of all." In Luke 22:25-26, Jesus is once again talking about "those who exercise authority". His comment is: "You are not to be like that. Instead, the greatest among you should be like the youngest, and the one who rules - like the one who serves." **It seems to me to be abundantly clear, even from these two remarks, that Jesus would not expect the leaders among His followers, to be "high profile". They were to be like the servants, hovering somewhere in the background, almost un-noticed!**

The disciples seem to have put this into practice in the Early Church. Nearly twenty years after his conversion, Paul went to Jerusalem to explain his "theology". He writes (in Galatians 2:2) "But I did this privately to those who seemed to be leaders" Paul! You amaze me! "Those who seemed to be leaders"! Years after the Church in Jerusalem is founded, is it still not clear who the leaders are? No - not immediately. Obviously there was no "official" leadership, or it would have been unmistakably clear to Paul who the leaders were. But once he had been there for some time, he began to realise which brothers the local believers particularly respected for their spiritual wisdom and their experience. A bit later in the same letter, Paul says it again: "James, Peter and John, those reputed to be pillars". (ch 2 v 9).

Leaders were often called "elders" in the Early Church. That word reflects a common practice of the day, throughout the Mediterranean world. In most communities, there were those who were recognised as the leaders, because of their experience and wisdom. Although age was a factor, it was not the only criterion for being an elder. Almost subconsciously, the people of a community would acknowledge who among them were their elders.

(I'm reminded of "The Admirable Crichton", an intriguing and amusing play by Scots writer J.M. Barrie. Set in the earlier part of the 20th century, it tells of an aristocratic family who become marooned on a desert island with their butler, housemaid, and one or two other staff. To begin with, everyone looks for leadership to Lord Loam, the hereditary head of the whole household; but as time passes, it becomes clear that the man who usually knows best in any situation is Crichton, the butler. Gradually people's attitudes change - including that of Lord Loam himself - and eventually the butler is the acknowledged leader of the stranded group. There is no election or appointment, It's just a fact of the life of their community.)

That is how elders often emerged in the communities of the ancient world. Of course, there were places where the choosing of elders was organised to suit people with influence, like the local big-wig, or a powerful family; or else an existing group of elders agreed to appoint their own successors. But, basically, it was "by common consent" throughout the locality. Those to whom the others turned often, for comment and advice - those were the elders. Sometimes that was recognised, officially, through an actual election, or an appointment by someone representing the King; sometimes the recognition was informal and unofficial.

So it was with the elders of the New Testament church. Acts 14:23 says - talking of the towns of Lystra, Iconium and Antioch -"Paul and Barnabas appointed elders for them in each church". The scholars seem to agree that the Greek text could just as easily mean "Paul and Barnabas had elders elected in each church" (In the NIV, it gives this alternative as a footnote.) Either way, there was, in these three towns, some kind of official appointment. Titus 1:5 shows that in Crete also there was official recognition. But, though there were elders everywhere, there is no other mention of apostles appointing elders, or of their being chosen "officially" by the other believers. Paul's talk of "those who seemed to be the leaders" suggests that it was equally acceptable **to have respected men who were unofficially or informally (even sub-consciously) recognised - but who were just as much elders.**

THAT'S HOW IT SEEMS TO ME TO BE DEVELOPING, AMONG THE "LOOSE ASSOCIATIONS". Leaders are "low-key", but after some time, you begin to know who they are.

* * * * * * * * * * * *

What did the New Testament elders actually do? Did they simply sit around until someone happened to ask for advice? No. They took initiative along a particular line. Think for a moment of leaders in areas of "Human Endeavour" (as opposed to leaders in Business or in Politics). I mean people like the Managers of Sports Teams, or the Heads of Expeditions, or even Parents within a Family. Leaders of such joint efforts have a clear task before them. They watch out, in a positive way, to see that the others put their best into whatever they are engaged in. They also see to it that the others **get the best out of** what they are engaged in. THAT WAS THE FUNCTION, I BELIEVE, OF THE NEW TESTAMENT ELDER: TO SEE THAT THE BELIEVERS GAVE THEIR BEST TO THE SERVICE OF CHRIST, AND THAT THEY GOT THE BEST OUT OF THEIR RELATIONSHIP WITH HIM.

There is a verse in Acts 20 which seems to me to summarise the function of elders. Addressing the ELDERS among the Christians at Ephesus, Paul says (verse 28): "Guard yourselves, and all the flock of which the Holy Spirit has made you OVERSEERS. Be SHEPHERDS of the church of God.." Of course, there are no block capitals in the original, but I put them there to highlight the two terms which are often interchanged with the term "Elder" - namely "Overseer" and "Shepherd". (These same three terms are interchanged also in 1 Peter 5:1-3)

An overseer is rather like the lifeguard on the top of his little ladder at the swimming pool. He has been given a raised-up position, but he is not "high-profile". You might hardly notice he was there, unless he saw it necessary to say or do something. **He is low-key, but vital.** He "watches over" the swimmers - alert to indicate facilities they might not be aware of; but also vigilant in case people break the rules of safety or consideration for others; and, of course, ready to get involved in any emergency.

A shepherd is rarely the actual owner of the sheep. But, on behalf of the owner, he sees to it that the sheep get everything they need, and also that their daily routine helps them to be as productive as possible, with regard to wool and meat.

ELDERS ARE TO SEE TO IT THAT BELIEVERS ARE AS PRODUCTIVE AS POSSIBLE, BUT ALSO THAT THEY ARE GETTING ALL THE RESOURCES CHRIST OFFERS TO HIS SERVANT-PEOPLE. THEY LIBERATE THE LOCAL CHRISTIANS INTO THE FULLNESS OF GOD'S GRACE, AND INTO FULLNESS OF SERVICE. AND IT IS EXACTLY THIS KIND OF LOW-KEY, UNOFFICIAL "OVERSEER" WHOM I AM BEGINNING TO OBSERVE AT WORK AMONG THOSE WHO ARE OUTSIDE THE USUAL CHURCH STRUCTURES!

CHAPTER 14

LEADERSHIP AND AUTHORITY

"Obey your leaders and submit to their authority" (Hebrews 13:17. At first sight *that* command does not seem to fit in with the informal, low-key pattern I have been describing! Even though the word "authority" is not actually in the original Greek of that verse, the use of terms like obey and submit seem fairly authoritarian! Does this verse not indicate something a bit stronger than my "overseer-in-the-background"? Does it not speak of some kind of "bosses" among us?

My first comment on that matter is that **Jesus laid down that there should be no "Boss-Man" arrangements among His followers!** In the previous chapter, I quoted Mark 10: 42-44: **"You know that their high officials exercise authority over them. NOT SO WITH YOU."** I have used bold print, and block capitals, to make sure no-one misses Jesus' startling comment. He is not in favour of Christian leaders exercising authority over the other believers! He says more or less the same thing in Luke 22:25-26. The result is that, whenever the New Testament uses words like "authority", "submission" or "obedience to leaders", we have to interpret these words in the light of what Jesus has clearly taught.

The full text of Hebrews 13:17 is this: "Obey your leaders and submit to their authority. They keep watch over you as men who must give an account. Obey them so that their work will be a joy, not a burden, for that would be of no advantage to you."

Here's how I interpret the verse. *Remembering what Jesus commanded about authority,* I suggest that the "authority" of these leaders must be like the authority of the staff at the swimming pool. The lifeguard/attendants certainly "keep watch over you". You know perfectly well that what they say and do is for everyone's "advantage". You would be stupid not to submit to any advice they think important enough to give. **They are usually just unobtrusive "overseers', but, should they think it necessary to give you a warning, or a very positive lead, you would have to have exceptionally good reasons for not obeying.**

That's how I see our response to those who are recognised as leaders in any group of Christians. That's the kind of response I note when "Admirable Crichtons" begin to emerge on the unstructured" scene. Naturally, you don't need to accept *my* interpretation of this "Obey your Leaders" verse, but however you view it, you must take into account Christ's ban on leaders being the same as "bosses".

I can see a genuine place, of course, for Organisers of specific projects - people in charge of a particular scheme, and with power to make decisions. We referred in both chapter 10 and chapter 12 to the seven men chosen to organise the distribution of food to those in need. (Praise God for Christians today who have "gifts of administration" which help to meet the vast practical needs which abound in the modern world.) The seven men of Acts 6 were "decision-makers" on behalf of the others - but their role was in the limited sphere of a particular worthwhile project. That is a very different matter from saying that a local body of Christians should be run by someone like a managing director, or by a group like a board-of-management.

* * * * * * * * * * * *

This is probably the place to add that I can also see a place for local leaders who can **teach** others. In 1 Timothy 3:2, Paul writes, "Now the overseer must be... able to teach". That's clear enough!

In another of his letters Paul uses a phrase which, in the Greek, is very much *one* idea - the phrase: "pastors-and-teachers" (Ephesians 4:11). Nowadays we would put a "stroke" between the two words to capture the right meaning: "pastor/teachers". Of course, the word "pastor" is simply an alternative way of translating "shepherd". So what Paul is saying is that Shepherds or Pastors or Overseers or Elders or Leaders (they're all the same!) should also be Instructors - just as the staff who oversee the swimming pool are usually also instructors.

I must stress, however, that there is nothing in the New Testament to suggest that the local "overseers" have all to be "Lecture-Style" teachers. There is no reason why most of them shouldn't work through "teaching-in-the-course-of-life". We went over all this in chapters 8 and 9. There is a need for *some* leaders who can address a whole group, if something fresh has to be passed on to everyone at the same time, or if there are enough novice Christians for teaching-a-group to be more practicable than one-to-one discipling. But the stated expectation of the Word of God is, simply, that local leaders should pass on what they have learned in the Scriptures, and in their experience of the Christian life. I cannot find any directives in Scripture about **how they** must do it.

Once again, what I observe, among those who have left the structures for a "house of living stones" does reflect this aspect of the Bible's picture of what a leader should be.

* * * * * * * * * * * *

However, let us return to considering Leadership in general, and let us draw our discussion of it to a conclusion. I wanted to point out that, in a strange way, the "job-description" which I have outlined for a Leader, is actually part of the job-description for every Christian! We have seen earlier that we are all to "encourage one another", all to "spur one another on to... good deeds" and all to "teach and admonish one another"! It is as everyone actually does that, that it begins to dawn on a Christian community that some people are specially gifted in this direction - some people have the hallmarks of leadership upon them.

Another way of putting that, is to say God's Spirit has given some people a heart for the care of fellow-believers. (Did you notice, in Acts 20:28, the phrase "Guard the flock, of which the **Holy Spirit** has made you overseers"?)

In New Testament times there didn't seem any need for those with a "pastoring-heart", or with leadership qualities, to get themselves formally recognised. It was no big deal. You did what the Lord laid on your heart, and if you *seemed*, to other people, to be gifted by the Holy Spirit as a leader - so be it! THAT'S HOW IT IS AMONG THE "HOUSE OF LIVING STONES" PEOPLE. So far, no-one has been able to convince me that, in the light of Scripture, our informal leadership-styles are out-of-order.

PART FOUR

DEALING WITH PEOPLE'S PRACTICAL RESERVATIONS

CHAPTER 15

MAINTAINING THE MOTIVATION

In 1 Corinthians 14:29, Paul teaches that we should "weigh carefully" what comes to us from other believers. You will realise by now, I am sure, that I have spent a good deal of time trying to "weigh" the unstructured church-lifestyle by comparing it with Scripture. For my own part, I am now quite satisfied that it is well within Biblical guidelines - firmly based on Biblical foundations. My studies have, in a sense, set me free, and strengthened my resolve to serve the Lord Jesus wholeheartedly within our new setting.

I am hoping that many others, who are also "outside the structures", will find, in what I have written, a confirmation of how they have been led themselves. I hope that they will be encouraged, and receive the kind of impetus that I have received.

I even dare to hope that some fellow-believers in "normal" churches will begin to realise that we are not, after all, weird heretics who are walking in error and delusion - but a perfectly valid expression of New Testament church-life. Happily, this has begun to happen within my own circle of Christian friends.

However, it is only fair to point out that even those who now agree that what we are doing is acceptable in principle, are still highly doubtful as to whether it has any hope of working out in practice! In these last few chapters I would like to look at some of their reservations in more detail.

One of the major practical reservations which I have heard expressed goes something like this: "I don't see myself surviving as an active Christian, let alone flourishing, if I were to cut myself off from the organised opportunities my church lays on for me - opportunities to receive teaching, to worship, to have fellowship, to serve others and to engage in evangelism. Are these activities not, in fact, vital 'support systems' for maintaining and motivating the Christian life?"

* * * * * * * * * *

There are three comments I would like to make about this kind of reservation. The first is that THE CHRISTIAN LIFE IS NOT REALLY MAINTAINED AND MOTIVATED BY 'SUPPORT SYSTEMS' BUT BY WHAT I CALL THE **DRIVE OF DISCIPLESHIP.** Whether you are inside the structures or outside them, you will only survive if you have that inner impetus which comes from being a committed disciple of Jesus.

Think for a moment about what it means to be the disciple of *any* master. **To be a disciple means that you set yourself to sit at the feet of that master** and get teaching from him. To be a disciple means that you set yourself to associate with other disciples of the same master. To be a disciple means that you admire and appreciate your master, and somehow you can't help expressing that appreciation. To be a disciple means that you set yourself to put your master's commands into operation daily, particularly any commands he specially emphasises. To be a disciple means that you are so convinced your master is the one everyone should relate to and follow, that you set yourself to be involved in bringing others to him. All this would apply to any kind of committed discipleship. It is certainly the nature of Christian discipleship. I am convinced that this is what Jesus is looking for in people who call themselves believers. I am convinced that this was what Jesus was talking about when He said "Go into all the world and make *disciples* of every nation".

If you are enthusiastically living out the Christian life in a "normal" church setting, it is actually that discipleship-attitude which motivates you - not the worship services, regular solid teaching, housegroups or organised Christian outreach. I could liken you to a railway train moving along the various tracks that are laid down for it. The tracks don't motivate the train! It can only be propelled forward by a driving force within it, although it uses the tracks to channel that driving force. Similarly, you may be working *through* the organisations and meetings your church lays on for you, but what really motivates you is the drive of discipleship within yourself.

My investigations, and my experience so far, tell me that this is exactly what motivates the Christians "outside the structures". That same sense of discipleship drives them to keep in touch with various sources of teaching. It drives them to build links with other Christians. It causes them to have worshipping hearts. It drives them to be constantly on the look-out for opportunities to serve others in Jesus' name. It causes them to seek to introduce others to the Lord. If you have been gripped by such a sense of discipleship, you *will* maintain the Christian life, come what may.

To return to my railway analogy: I have suspected recently that God is looking for new "forms of transport" to carry His grace to a needy world - that He may be raising up what one might call "aircraft-Christians" as well as "railway-train-Christians"! Trains operate under the system of having something *constructed* for them, to channel their movements - but aircraft operate without such structures. Can you really say that trains, because they use structures, are a *better* form of transport than planes? So long as planes are propelled forward, are guided and directed by Air Traffic Control, and are carrying the cargo their owner wants, they are serving their purpose. AND SO LONG AS CHRISTIANS OUTSIDE THE STRUCTURES ARE MOTIVATED BY THAT DRIVE OF DISCIPLESHIP, AND GUIDED AND DIRECTED BY THE HOLY SPIRIT, THEY WILL SERVE GOD'S PURPOSES.

This analogy is, I believe, worth thinking about. My first comment, then, on your claim that you couldn't see yourself surviving without the well-tried "support systems" of normal church life is this: Multitudes of Christians would survive perfectly well if God called them outside the structures - because they are *disciples* of Jesus, very much in the mould described earlier in this chapter.

*   *   *   *   *   *   *   *   *   *   *   *

Sadly, however, there are also multitudes of Christians who would not survive if, somehow or other, they found themselves "outside the structures". This is because, through the ages, a great deal of Christian work has produced "**institution-dependent**" **believers** - folks who might be described as "**church-propelled**" rather than as "**discipleship-propelled**".

Such Christians do get teaching, but it is because their church has arranged a teaching programme for them - rather than because of an inner spirit of discipleship which positively desires to sit at the feet of Jesus. They do get fellowship, but it is because their church lays it on for them and constantly urges them to take advantage of it - rather than because something within motivates them to seek out the company of other followers-of-Jesus for mutual encouragement. They are engaged in Christian service, but it is because their church has arranged channels of service, and exhorted them to be involved - rather than because they have a personal vision of blessing others in Jesus' name. They are "church-propelled" rather than "discipleship-propelled". They are "institution-dependent".

You may think that I am being unduly cynical, or that I am making a fuss about nothing - but history and experience have shown that there is a whole range of ways in which God allows Christians to be cut off from their institutions. It looks as if, at various times and places, He tests the Church to see whether Jesus' final order (to make disciples) is being put into operation; or whether the Church has been content to make more superficial converts.

Take, for instance, the situation - all too common over the centuries - where a hostile government, in a particular country, has banned all Christian meetings and dismantled all church organisations. Such an eventuality reveals who the real disciples are and who have just been carried along by the good arrangements or the good fellowship.

Evangelism is supposed to involve fishers-of-men bringing real live fish into the Kingdom; but when a hostile government comes down heavily on Christianity, it often turns out that many of the Christians are, when the crunch comes, more like pieces of wood carried along by the current of the church stream, than like healthy fish with an inner motivation to swim in the right direction. The reason the Chinese Church survived and grew, during the Communist regime, was that it was imbued by just that sense of discipleship I have been describing - but throughout history that kind of outcome has been the exception rather than the rule.

It doesn't require a political catastrophe, however, to cut Christians off from their institutions. It can happen in the most ordinary of circumstances. Take the case of the young person who becomes a Christian, and is nurtured, in what he or she considers a "wonderful" church. The worship is wonderful; the teaching is wonderful; the fellowship is wonderful. Then one day that young person's father announces that, for reasons connected with his work, the family will be moving to another part of the country. It turns out that there is no "wonderful" church within easy reach in the new area. Does the young person survive as an active Christian? That depends. If a spirit of discipleship has been positively fostered in the original church, then, of course, an active Christian life continues. But if the young person has merely been swept along by everything that was wonderful, then an active Christian life won't last long.

Unfortunately, the latter result is all too common - and not just among young people. The aim should *not* be to link people to a wonderful church; it should be to link people to a wonderful Lord. A wonderful church may be a bonus, but it is not sufficient basis for Christian growth and perseverance. The only basis for *that* is a real sense of discipleship.

I could give many other examples of situations where reliance on institutions has had a detrimental effect on believers when they are separated from these institutions. But I hope I have already said enough to get across the point that SOME CHRISTIANS ARE CHURCH-PROPELLED, INSTEAD OF BEING DISCIPLESHIP-PROPELLED.

That fact has special relevance to the growth of the unstructured churches. People sometimes ask me if I am advocating that everyone leaves their existing churches and gets into the unstructured scene. My answer is: definitely not! As I have said before, I don't believe anyone should be making such a life-changing move without a clear sense of call from God. I now want to add this: You should not consider such a call to be *confirmed*, unless you have a strong awareness of the drive of discipleship within yourself.

If there are Christians who honestly believe they *don't* have that inner drive, I would not think they need feel personally guilty about it. They are the victims of certain styles of evangelism, or of leadership which has made participation-in-church-activities the thermometer for commitment to Christ. They should be encouraged to know that it is possible to rise above the system, and to re-direct their lives along discipleship lines, whether inside or outside the structures. If they are contemplating leaving "normal" church life, they should not cut loose, from the structures on which they have become dependent, until they sense that they have become "discipleship-propelled".

There is another way in which the whole issue of "institution-dependent" Christians is relevant to the subject of this book. If God wants to build local churches which don't breed "institution-dependency", but which stimulate personal discipleship, a very viable way of doing it would be to build churches which don't actually have any institutions! For this reason I can see why **house-of-living-stones churches** might well be very much within God's plans for the future, as He seeks to develop sturdy discipleship.

This would be specially important if, as many evangelical and charismatic Christians are saying, the "End Times" are approaching. If that is the case, there is tribulation and persecution ahead for the Church. Under these circumstances, I don't see hostile authorities leaving the Church's structures and institutions neatly in place. They will pull them down! *Organised* church life will be hopelessly disrupted! I SOMETIMES SUSPECT THAT GOD IS RAISING UP THE UNSTRUCTURED CHURCH TO WITHSTAND THE CHAOS OF THE END TIMES.

Those who are outside the structures should not feel any pride in the importance that God may be attaching to their lifestyle. They should see it as an awesome challenge. They must pay close attention to constantly nurturing that inward sense of discipleship, in themselves and in their fellow "outsiders".

* * * * * * * * * *

The last of my three comments on the so-called "support systems" (the customs and institutions which have grown up round Christ's commands to His church) is: not only can they weaken discipleship if not kept in proper perspective, but **they can also discourage people from becoming Christians in the first place!**

If you become a Christian through any particular church, or grouping of churches, you seem to have to take on board a lot more than just Jesus Himself! You are clearly expected to take on the ways of that church, or at least of some church. You are clearly expected to be involved in some form of institutional life. Many open-hearted people have a gut-reaction against this. Without being able to put it into words, they want "to be themselves in the Lord". But that is very difficult in the institutionalised churches. You do not become, merely, a Christian. You more or less have to become a particular type of Christian. This puts a lot of people off, including the children of believers as they grow into adults. Many honest folk are not really against responding to Jesus, but cannot bring themselves to respond to what they have experienced of churches.

The problem is not nearly so acute in the unstructured churches. The Christians there would still need to spell out that you don't have to become cloned to any characteristics the local "outsiders" happen to share - but there is no institutional package involved in your relationship with Christ in that scene. I have become convinced that "being yourself in the Lord" is much easier when the institutions are stripped away.

All this has led me to suspect that yet another reason why God seems to be raising up an "Unstructured Church" is that He wants to present to the world **Jesus only** - not Jesus-plus-a-whole-package- of-institutions-and-ways-of-doing-things.

Once again, this is not a compliment to those outside the structures, but a staggering challenge!

*   *   *   *   *   *   *   *   *   *

I suppose I began this chapter trying to justify a lack of organised "support systems" in the life of the unstructured churches. I have ended up being more convinced than ever that the Lord has great purposes ahead for those outside the structures. If they respond to the challenge, they can present an un-institutionalised Jesus to the world; they can train up believers who, though highly valuing the support of other Christians, don't live in any state of dependency (except on the Lord); and they can be "airplane" Christians, unfettered by specific ways of doing things - with a unique potential to "mount up with eagles' wings".

CHAPTER 16

INVOLVED IN FRUITFULNESS

There is another approach which those who have grave doubts about our unstructured lifestyle tend to make. It goes something like this:

"I grant you that 'the structures' *do* get in the way, but at least they have produced some fruit over the years. However you define 'fruitfulness', most normal churches have got *something* to show for their labours, and some churches have achieved a great deal. So far as those 'outside the structures' are concerned, I really don't see much that you could call 'fruit' - and Jesus says 'By their fruit you shall know them'."

Christians who think along these lines sometimes emphasise their point by contrasting us with some highly successful churches they know of. There are, at any given time, reports from various parts of the world about churches which are growing by leaps and bounds; churches where the believers (including many young people) are obviously deeply dedicated to serving God; churches which are organised to be involved with many serious areas of need.

"In comparison with such dynamic churches," people tend to say, "your flimsy networks of unorganised Christians - your feeble 'loose associations' - seem rather pathetic. If we want something to aim at in church-lifestyle, it would be those wonderfully successful churches, and not your vague and untested ways!"

As I have read the Bible over the years, however, three aspects of fruitfulness have impressed themselves upon me. I believe these three emphases are worth considering by all Christians, whatever their situation - but I also believe they will help my readers towards a better understanding of those outside the structures.

* * * * * * * * * * * *

The first point is this: FRUITFULNESS ALWAYS NEEDS TIME TO DEVELOP. DON'T DESPISE THE EARLY STAGES OF THE PROCESS.

If you look through all the Biblical references to fruitfulness (or to Harvest) you will build up a picture of a great many preliminary stages leading up to the glorious harvesting of the crops or the fruit. The following may not be a complete list but it gives some idea of what I'm talking about: 1. Ploughing (or breaking up the hard ground); 2. Removing Stones; 3. Sowing Seed; 4. Watering; 5. Weeding; 6. Hoeing (i.e. digging round plants or trees which are already growing); 7. Fertilising;

and, finally, 8. Patient Waiting (for the plant to go through *its* stages of development).

If you agree that this process is outlined in the Bible, you can jump immediately to the next full paragraph. If you have doubts, then here are some of the scriptures which have given me this impression: "My loved one had a vineyard on a fertile hillside. He dug it up and cleared it of stones and planted it with choicest vines."(Isaiah 5:1-2). "Sir," the man replied (to the dissatisfied owner of a fig tree), "leave it alone for one more year, and I'll dig round it, and fertilise it." (Luke 13:8). "I planted the seed, Apollos watered it, but God made it grow." (1 Corinthians 3:6). The famous "Parable of the Sower" hints that weeding might usefully have been done: "Other seed fell among thorns which grew up and choked the plants so that they did not bear grain." (Mark 4:7). "All by itself the soil produces corn - first the stalk, then the ear, then the full kernel." (Mark 4:28).

Some Christians seem to give great honour to individuals, or to bodies of believers, who have reached a "harvest stage", and rather to despise those who are at an earlier stage in the process. The Bible, on the other hand, seems to give equal honour to everyone who is genuinely engaged in doing God's work, no matter at what stage they are - e.g. "The man who plants and the man who waters have one purpose, and each will be rewarded according to his own labour." (1 Corinthians 3:8). (Jesus even teaches that, sometimes at least, great fruitfulness is the result of the labours of others, and not of those who are actually involved in the harvest: "I sent you to reap what you have not worked for. Others have done the hard work, and you have reaped the benefits of their labour." (John 4:38).)

THIS "PROCESS OF FRUITFULNESS" TEACHING IS WORTH REMEMBERING BY ALL CHRISTIANS. **It should help those who feel they have been "successful" to remain in an attitude of humility.** They could be reaping what others have sown. And even if their fruitfulness is, in a manner of speaking, "all their own work", they should recognise that, while they themselves have reached the final stage of a process, others may well be working faithfully (and "successfully") at an earlier stage. Similarly, **it should counteract discouragement among those who serve the Lord to the fullness of what has been revealed to them, and yet do not seem, at the moment, to see "results".**

My main purpose, however, in reminding you of this biblical concept of "the process of fruitfulness", is its relevance to the growing church-outside-the-structures. Many of the practical criticisms I hear of our unstructured ways are examples of not giving something new a reasonable time to develop. For instance, folk say: "I don't see many young people involved in this" or "I don't see many new converts-to-Christ through their views on outreach" or "Only a tiny minority of Christians think like them". Listen to Zechariah 4:10: "Who despises the day of small things?" If God is doing something special by building up loose associations of dedicated Christians (as I believe He is) the work is clearly only in its early stages -

and, as such, is not to be despised.

BE ASSURED THAT, IF THIS CHANGED EMPHASIS IN CHURCH LIFE IS FROM THE LORD, THE WHOLE THING WILL GROW AND GROW - IN HIS GOOD TIME AND IN HIS OWN WAY.

* * * * * * * * * * * *

The second comment I have to make about fruitfulness is this: IN THE LAST ANALYSIS, THERE IS ONLY ONE HUMAN RESPONSE WHICH CAN LEAD TO FRUITFULNESS - AND "UNSTRUCTURED" CHRISTIANS ARE JUST AS CAPABLE OF MAKING THAT RESPONSE AS "STRUCTURED" ONES.

The response I am talking about has two parts to it, but it is a connected whole. I call it: listen-and-obey. Let me illustrate and explain...

There are occasions when I find myself having to serve a meal to guests in our home, as Mavis, my wife, is sometimes unavailable. (It so happens that I had to do it yesterday, which is why this analogy came to mind!) When I serve a meal, I am almost always highly complimented! So I have to confess: actually, it was Mavis who did nearly everything! All I had to do was to listen carefully to her instructions, and then simply put them into operation. She has planned the meals, done the shopping, prepared the dishes for the cooker or the microwave, and left guidelines about the trimmings! It is true that the guests wouldn't get the benefit of the meal if I didn't play my part - but it would be quite wrong for me to take the credit for the blessing they say they receive!

That household illustration seems to me to explain the relationship between the work God does and the work He expects Christians to do. The Bible emphasises that it is God who brings about fruitfulness; it is the grace-of-God which accomplishes His good things on earth. And yet, there is a clearly defined part for His people to play - to listen to His instructions and then to carry them out. Let the Scriptures speak for themselves:

"Praise to the Lord God, the God of Israel, who <u>alone</u> does marvellous deeds" (Psalm 72:18). "<u>The Lord</u> has done this, and it is marvellous in our eyes" (Psalm 118:23). "'Not by might, nor by power, but <u>by my Spirit', says the Lord Almighty</u>" (Zechariah 4:6). "Let him who boasts, boast in <u>the Lord</u>" (1 Cor.1:31; 2 Cor.10:17). "Neither he who plants nor he who waters is anything, but <u>only God</u>, who makes things grow" (1 Cor.3:7). The words of Peter, explaining the successful healing of the lame beggar at the gate of the Temple, can be applied to all real "success" in Christian circles: "Why does this surprise you? Why do you stare at us, **as if by our <u>own</u> power or godliness we had made this (happen)?** <u>The God of our fathers</u> has glorified His servant Jesus" (Acts 3:12,13).

The Old and New Testaments are quite clear that when good things happen in

Kingdom-Life - when there is a fruitful harvest - the Lord has brought it about.

On the other hand, the Bible also gives an important place to the part played in the "success" by God's servants - the continuous response of listening-and-obeying.

When God spoke to Joshua as the Israelites prepared to enter the Promised Land, it was listening-and-obeying which He stressed: "Be careful to <u>obey</u> all the law my servant Moses gave you... that you might be successful wherever you go.. <u>Meditate on it day and night</u> so that you may be careful to do everything written in it" (Joshua 1:7,8) (Notice that the word "success" is mentioned in connection with the "listening-and-obeying" principle.)

Samuel added the concept of the Voice-of-the-Lord to the concept of the Written-Law when he spoke about listening-and-obeying: "Does the Lord delight in burnt offerings and sacrifices as much as in <u>obeying the voice of the Lord</u>? To <u>obey</u> is better than sacrifice, and to <u>heed</u> is better than the fat of rams (1 Samuel 15:22).

Jesus taught: "Everyone who <u>hears these words of mine, and puts them into practice</u>, is like a wise man who built his house upon the rock" (Matthew 7:24).

Listening-and-obeying is the human side of what brings about fruitfulness. I believe that it is close attention to Christ's step-by-step instructions which produces what Jesus calls "fruit that will last" (John 15:16).

NOW, IS THERE ANY PARTICULAR REASON WHY THE CHRISTIANS "OUTSIDE THE STRUCTURES" ARE LESS ABLE TO FOLLOW THIS SIMPLE PROCEDURE OF LISTENING-AND-OBEYING THAN CHRISTIANS WITHIN THE USUALLY ACCEPTED CHURCH STRUCTURES? I DO NOT THINK SO!

My experience of these "unstructured" folks tells me that they are very much the kind of people who take the direction of the written Word-of-God seriously - and the kind of people to whom the personal leading of the Holy Spirit is a reality. It is not at all true that they have a "ghetto-mentality" - that they "keep themselves to themselves" and have no awareness of what God might be saying, prophetically, to other Christians. They <u>do</u> get to know what "winds of doctrine" are blowing nowadays. They will "weigh" these, of course, and ask whether they, personally, are meant to respond. They will not be "blown about by every wind of doctrine", but they will be aware of the possibilities. **SO FAR AS I CAN TELL, THEY ARE LISTENING-AND-OBEYING PEOPLE - AND, AS SUCH, ARE ON COURSE TO BE INVOLVED IN THE FRUITFUL THINGS GOD DOES.**

For my own part, I actually find it easier, nowadays, to concentrate on that simple procedure of listening-and-obeying, and to make it the focus of my being, than I did when my life was largely prearranged by quite a demanding schedule of church activities. More and more I can say "What next, Lord?", without having to consult my diary! I sense an ability, personally, to be more "in step with the Spirit"; a new freedom to be fruitful in what God wants of me.

* * * * * * * * * * * *

The final aspect of fruitfulness which I want to comment on is this: GOD SEEMS TO DELIGHT IN USING WHAT APPEARS, TO HUMAN EYES, TO BE FEEBLE AND LACKING-IN-POTENTIAL, TO BRING ABOUT HIS PURPOSES! "The stone the builders rejected has become the Capstone" (Psalm 118:22). I realise that Jesus applied this verse to Himself, but it describes a principle the Lord often uses. He chose Bethlehem as the place for Jesus to be born - even though most people thought it was "the least of the cities of Judah". He chose Galilee as the place for Jesus to be brought up - even though most people thought, "Can any good thing come out of Galilee?".

The apostle Paul confirms the principle: "God chose the foolish things of the world to shame the wise. God chose the weak things of the world to shame the strong. He chose the lowly things of this world and the despised things - and the things that are not - to nullify the things that are" (1 Cor. 1:27,28).

So, let no one underestimate our "flimsy networks of unorganised Christians". God is quite capable of choosing "things that are not" - things without form or structure - to bear fruit for Him. He is quite able to do His mighty work through nothing more than Houses of Living Stones.

* * * * * * * * * * * *

IF THE CHRISTIANS OF THE "UNSTRUCTURED CHURCH" CONTINUE TO LISTEN-AND-OBEY, THERE IS ABSOLUTELY NO REASON WHY THEY SHOULD NOT BE WONDERFULLY INVOLVED IN THE VARIOUS STAGES OF THE FRUITFUL THINGS GOD WILL DO IN THE TIME THAT LIES AHEAD.

CHAPTER 17

A VISION OF THE BODY OF CHRIST?

There is one final group of practical objections which has still to be considered. It has been suggested that though we highly value the scripture-based phrase "house of living stones", we neglect the equally biblical phrase "the body of Christ". "These living-stones people may relate well to one another" say our detractors, "but they don't act in any co-ordinated way. The parts of the body may indeed be linked firmly together, but there is little evidence of such a local church acting as a unified body. The whole thing is far too individualistic".

For instance, the very last verse of the book of Judges (ch.21:25 AV) is often used as a kind of well-meant accusation against us: "Everyone did what was right in his own eyes". "That's your unstructured believers!", say those who are worried about us, "Not fitting in with any church! Doing their own thing! Picking and choosing what suits them! In fact, just doing what is right in their own eyes!"

Why do people only quote half the sentence? The full sentence says this: "In those days, Israel had no king; everyone did what was right in his own eyes." **This verse does not apply to "unstructured" Christians, because they do have a king - a King whose commands, by the Word and the Spirit, they take very seriously indeed.** The verse doesn't apply to any committed believer. The only possible modern application would be to unbelievers who don't acknowledge Jesus as King.

When people misuse this verse with regard to Christians outside the structures, what they are really objecting to, I think, is that these Christians are obeying the Lord **directly** rather than obeying Him **through church-leaders.** I have already explained (in chapters 13 and 14) that leaders have a very real contribution to make in showing believers if there is something unbiblical about the guidance they think they are getting from the Lord. But that is a very different thing from saying that the leaders are the ones who should be giving the guidance. The common practice of leaders directing members, and launching initiatives on behalf of the whole local church, is, when you really think about it, a great distortion of the doctrine of the Body of Christ!

I must admit, however, that I only gradually realised this over a period of twenty years. For fifteen of these years I was "in the Ministry" - I was a "Pastor" (in the sense usually accepted in traditional evangelical churches). During that time I experienced, on several occasions, the very uncomfortable feeling that the particular local "Body of Christ" with which I was associated, was like a man **with two heads!** It had *Christ* to take initiative and issue orders - but it also had *me* ! Of course, I wasn't taking the lead totally independently. There were "elders" and "deacons" who shared the responsibility. Nevertheless, the local believers had *two* sources of leadership and initiative!

The theory seemed to be (though there was nothing in Scripture to back this up) that those of us in the leadership-team were like the central-nervous-system of the body: not really issuing instructions or suggestions ourselves, but simply transmitting messages from the Head. The problem was that, though some very positive things did develop, many so-called initiatives came to nothing or next-to-nothing - giving me the distinct impression that they had had their origin in *us* and had not truly come from the Head. I came to the conclusion that, in many matters, *I myself* had tried to lead (within the whole leadership team). The Body had at least two Heads - one divine *and* one human. Numerous conversations with other leaders of various types, over the years, have convinced me that this "spiritual schizophrenia" is a problem in many a local "Body of Christ".

Things seemed better for a while when I left the ministry and joined a Charismatic Fellowship, eventually being appointed a "leader" there too. In the early days there did seem to be a sense of the "members" relating directly to the Head, and the Holy Spirit co-ordinating everyone's leading into a rather wonderful pattern. But as the years passed, throughout most of the "Charismatic Movement", leadership teams seemed, on the whole, to develop a need to organise; to launch initiatives; to dig channels for people to operate along; to do all the things leadership has always done in the more traditional churches. **Once again I began to get, now with increasing frequency, this grotesque picture of our local Body-of-Christ (which I was partly influencing) being like a man with more than one head.**

IF AN ORDINARY BODY WORKS BY EACH MEMBER BEING LINKED DIRECTLY TO THE HEAD WITHOUT ANY INTERMEDIARY SOURCE OF INSTRUCTION OR DIRECTION, WHY SHOULD THE BODY-OF-CHRIST NOT WORK LIKE THAT TOO?

* * * * * * * * * * * *

There seem to me to be two reasons why leaders, admittedly with the best of intentions, feel the need to intervene, and act as "intermediary-heads". The first reason appears to be the notion that the average Christian needs a lot of teaching (decades of teaching, perhaps!) before he can be trusted to hear the voice of the Lord for himself. But is that idea really true to Scripture? Consider Jesus' words about His ordinary sheep, in John 10: "The man who enters by the gate is the shepherd of his sheep... and the sheep listen to his voice. He calls his own sheep by name, and leads them out.. They follow him because they know his voice. I am the good shepherd... I have other sheep who are not of this sheep pen.. They too will listen to my voice ....My sheep listen to my voice; I know them, and they follow me." (John 10:1-4, 14,16,27.) It seems that Jesus expects His "ordinary sheep" to be able to hear His voice, and follow the directions He gives to each one personally.

I can't help thinking of Ananias of Damascus. He was an "ordinary" believer, if ever there was one. We never hear of him before Acts 9:10 - and he passes out of the record book nine verses later! He was also a *new* believer, for this was at the very beginning of the Christian church in his home city. And yet he heard the voice of the Lord in a clear and detailed way, and was able to be involved in catapulting Saul of Tarsus into Christian service.

Of course it's true that, as individual "sheep", we will not *always* get our guidance right. In this earthly existence, as the famous chapter 13 of 1 Corinthians points out, we "see through a glass darkly". (It should be noted that church-leaders have not always got it right either. It causes much more trouble when a leader, or a group of leaders, sends a whole body of believers off at a tangent, than when an individual fails to hear correctly, and affects a much more limited sphere.) The job of leaders is *not* to give everyone else the Lord's guidance because they can't hear it for themselves, but simply to help individuals to be certain that what they have heard is truly from the Lord. I believe it is **biblical, and realistic in practice, to put much more trust in the ability of the ordinary Christian to hear the voice of the Lord for himself.**

Another reason why leaders seem to intrude into the natural (or, you could say, supernatural) functioning of the Body-of-Christ is the feeling that CO-ORDINATION is needed - that someone must co-ordinate the efforts of local Christians. But, is that not the function of the Holy Spirit? I have read through the Acts of the Apostles again and again, and I can only conclude that the Holy Spirit masterminded the whole thing! I don't see human strategies and initiatives. As I said earlier, I see "pockets" of human organisation (usually connected with the practical outworking of blessing the needy in material ways), but the growth of Kingdom-Life is brought about by the Holy Spirit. There is nothing "hit-and-miss" about the way the Spirit organises things. Jesus said "I will build my church" - but everyone seems to expect human leaders to do the job for Him. I believe it is biblical, and realistic in practice, to put much more trust in the ability of the Holy Spirit to bring about Kingdom-Life in our midst.

Ephesians 4 has an interesting short passage about the Body of Christ which I think is worth adding to what I quoted about leadership in chapters 13 and 14 of this book. "Speaking the truth in love, we will in all things grow up into Him who is the Head, that is Christ. From Him the whole body, joined and held together by every supporting ligament, grows and builds itself up in love, as each part does its work" (Eph. 4:15-16). Bearing in mind everything else the New Testament says about leadership, I don't think it is unreasonable to suggest that leaders among any group of Christians, if they are to be likened to any part of the body, could be called supporting ligaments, holding the parts of the Body to the Head and to each other.

We already saw that their task was to check, in a positive way, that their brothers and sisters were keeping in touch with the Lord, and following His personal lead for themselves - while, at the same time trying to ensure that everything which could helpfully flow from the Head to the "member" was actually flowing. We already saw that *everyone* has that task with relation to one another, but the Holy Spirit particularly lays the responsibility on some people whom we eventually recognise as "leaders". If it helps to assign a body-part to leaders, you could say: LEADERS ARE LIKE LIGAMENTS! LEADERS CERTAINLY AREN'T TO BE LIKE HEADS - OTHERWISE THE BODY WILL BE A MONSTROSITY. CHRIST IS TO BE THE SOLE HEAD.

* * * * * * * * * * * *

Because the Church of Jesus Christ has been so organised over the centuries, it is difficult for Christian people to realise all this. Organisations need Organisers, and it is understandable - though very regrettable - that leaders begin to feel they must fulfil the duties of a Managing Director (if they are in sole charge) or of a Board of Management (if there is shared leadership). Don't blame the leaders too much, however. All this is the underlying expectation of Christian people in general.

This was the issue which, above all, left me open to be drawn into the church-without-structures. It does not seem so difficult there to look on Christ as the only Head, while still appreciating the comments and example of the "elders" who gradually emerge. PEOPLE HAVE BEEN SAYING THAT THOSE OF US WHO HAVE LEFT THE "NORMAL" CHURCHES HAVE A POOR CONCEPT OF THE LOCAL BODY OF CHRIST. I WOULD SAY THAT WE HAVE A CLEAR AND ACCURATE CONCEPT!

We see Jesus looking down on *all* the Christians in an area, and considering them as His local Body. We see Him wanting to coordinate them all by His Holy Spirit alone, weaving their care for others, and their witness to others, into a perfect pattern. We see Him valuing the awareness each "member" has of the other, and the contribution of the special encouragers or "overseers". But we see Him wanting each member to relate directly to Himself, to hear and obey His voice, and not to be diverted by any leadings which are actually only of human origin. He wants to be Lord of all the local Christians, without intermediaries.

All this may seem unrealistic and naive in the present church climate, not only because of all the *organisations* involved, but also because of all the *denominations* involved. I remember a situation, a few years ago, when our family was one of three active Christian families living next door to one another. Each family was associated with a different local church, and yet, even in those days, I could not believe we were members of a different Body, *in Christ's eyes*. I am sure that there are many Christians who, in their heart of hearts, share this conviction. God's fullest purpose would be to co-ordinate every Christian in a given area to function as one - to accomplish His will in the area.

Could this ever come about? Could such a transformation ever take place in the world-wide Church? Could the Body of Christ ever become solely Christ-directed again? I suggest to you that it *could* happen if the Lord began to form local bodies with these characteristics - local bodies which grew in themselves, and were duplicated over and over again elsewhere. **I humbly suggest to you that that is what may well be happening in the appearance and spread of unstructured churches - the Lord building churches in which the members look to Him as sole Head.**

(A word of warning: no human being should try to build such churches. It has to be the Lord's doing - as His Spirit draws one and another to focus on Himself, and then links them with each other.)

*   *   *   *   *   *   *   *   *   *

All through this book I have been arguing that the unstructured churches - the "houses of living stones" - which are gradually appearing all over the place, are well within biblical guidelines - but it wouldn't surprise me if they are much more than just an alternative Christian lifestyle.

It wouldn't surprise me if the unstructured churches are the beginning of a great move by God to re-form the Body of Christ, with Jesus as its sole Head and Director, a universal Church unblemished by human contrivances.

It wouldn't surprise me if the unstructured churches turn out to be stepping-stones to the church of the future; the church of the new millennium; the flexible church which is needed to withstand the pressures of the end times.

It wouldn't surprise me if the unstructured churches are the logical follow-on from the Charismatic Renewal which, for a season at any rate, seemed to demonstrate that, if you "keep in step with the Spirit", rather than follow various human patterns, great things come about.

To those of you who have been critical of the Christians who have "left the structures" may I say this final word: It may be justifiable for you to find fault with individuals in that lifestyle, or with specific aspects of the lifestyle. But beware lest it is mere <u>customs</u> which you are so rigorously defending and not <u>commands</u>. And beware, even more, of **dismissing too readily what may well be a vital move of God in the working out of His purposes**

To those of you who are already moving with Christ outside the structures I would say this (as I say it to myself): Continue to sail in the uncharted seas. The Pilot Himself has the maps and the plans. Keep close to Him by listening-and-obeying. Reach out to bless your fellow believers. Reach out to bless your fellow human-beings in every possible way. Have expectancy and confidence in the Lord. Know that you are involved in something very good - something very much in line with His

Word. And know that He is able to do exceeding abundantly, above all that we ask or think. AMEN. LET IT BE SO.

Further copies of this book can be obtained by contacting any of the distributors below. If writing, please mark "Custom and Command" clearly on your envelope. The book is offered free of charge, but a contribution to postage and packaging is appreciated.

In the United Kingdom:	Mr and Mrs J. S. Firth, c/o 2c, Gander Green Lane, SUTTON, Surrey, SM1 2EH.
In the Republic of Ireland:	Mr and Mrs David Rice, 37, Marley Walk, Rathfarnham, DUBLIN 16. e-mail: drice@tinet.ie
In New Zealand	Mr and Mrs John Beaumont, 83a, Cottonwood Street, Parklands, CHRISTCHURCH 9.
In the Republic of South Africa:	Mr and Mrs Guy Dennison, 38 Eland Road, ROBINHILLS 2194, Tel. (011) 793-7294
In the United States of America	Mr and Mrs Wally Duguid, Po Box 472 SHAKOPEE MN 55379 e-mail: duguid@compuserve.com or wduguid@bgea.org